PRAISE FOR *ITERATE*

"There are lots of books out there talking about 'change' in education. However, Justin has written one of the few, if not the only one, that talks honestly about the negatives of 'top-down' change being done 'to' teachers and students, and points the way to 'bottom-up' change done 'with' teachers, students, and their families."

—**Larry Ferlazzo**, high school educator, author, and
EducationWeek teacher advice columnist

"I wish I had a red telephone in my office that I could pick up any time I wanted to talk with Justin Reich about the beautiful, sticky, and crucial work of helping schools evolve. This book will now sit on my desk and play the role of that phone. *Iterate* is packed with thoughtful perspectives, real stories, and actionable approaches for how we can create the conditions for positive change in schools. And it's all shared in a crisp conversational tone with vibrant illustrations. I never have to call Justin again!"

—**Sam Seidel**, co-author of *Hip Hop Genius 2.0* and
Creative Hustle and K12 Lab Director of Strategy +
Research at the Stanford School

"Perhaps the greatest praise I can give a new book is this: I want to give this to all my educator friends and colleagues. There is so much in this book that 'works'! I found myself repeatedly saying, 'Yes! Yes! I agree with that! Yes, that makes so much sense!' Here's one: 'If we want students to try new ideas, teachers must do so, too.' Or this one, 'Design as flare and focus,' or, even more powerful: the idea of having more adults in schools who still teach part-time. And the best, 'only teachers can change teaching and learning.' There are so many invaluable nuggets of wisdom and truth in this book. Better still, most of it is available for free through Creative Commons. Reich has given the field an important and exciting new resource."

—**Linda Nathan**, lecturer at the Harvard Graduate School of Education and founding head of Boston Arts Academy

"Justin Reich stands out as one of the most brilliant minds in education reform. In his latest book *Iterate: The Secret to Innovation in Schools*, he masterfully combines his extensive academic research and vast experience as an educator to create an immensely useful resource for guiding change in schools. This book offers an invaluable blend of concepts, strategies, and tools that empower school leaders and individuals to understand and effectively design innovation within educational communities."

—**Tom Daccord**, co-founder of EdTechTeacher

"In *Iterate: The Secret to Innovation in Schools*, Reich masterfully synthesizes decades of research and practice into a powerful set of strategies that help spark change in education. Acknowledging that schools are complex systems that operate on many levels, the three practical and ready-to-implement approaches shared in this book demonstrate how to engage all stakeholders in collaborative experimentation that works!"

—**Tom Driscoll**, CEO of EdTechTeacher

"In *The Magic School Bus*, Ms. Frizzle gives her students some great advice: 'Take chances, make mistakes, get messy.' In his timely new book *Iterate*, Justin Reich gives similar advice for classroom teachers and school leaders, providing useful examples and practical tips on how to innovate at all levels of the school ecosystem by continually experimenting with new approaches and making changes based on the results, over and over again."

—**Mitch Resnick**, professor at MIT; director of the Lifelong Kindergarten group at the MIT Media Lab; and developer of the Scratch creative computing community

"*Iterate* is more than a guide—it's an irresistible call to action for educators, leading toward innovation and systemic transformation. Reich, with his impressive wisdom drawn from profound involvement in educational reform, weaves compelling narratives that make this book a captivating journey. Rich in research-based practices, this work is not merely about reading cover to cover, but about learning, applying, and iterating upon the myriad lessons and practical strategies it imparts. An essential compass in the pursuit of educational metamorphosis, *Iterate* masterfully turns insights into action."

—**Eric Klopfer**, professor at MIT and director
of the Scheller Teacher Education Program

"Reich by no means underestimates the challenges and complexity of promoting innovation in schools and what it can require of teachers and school leaders. But this is a hope inspiring, energizing book that will be immensely helpful for all educators who are trying to roll up their sleeves and get on with exploring, prototyping, trying, reflecting— and iterating on—the kinds of locally responsive improvements to teaching and learning that all students need and deserve. Reich deftly and coherently steers the reader through a plethora of ideas—some well-known and some his own—that can be tried out on Monday within a single classroom or used to inform large-scale, systemic change."

—**Liz Dawes Duraisingh**, co-director and principal
investigator at Project Zero; lecturer at Harvard Graduate
School of Education; and author of *Inquiry-Driven Innovation:
A Practical Guide to Supporting School-Based Change*

"Justin Reich has written a gem of a book. *Iterate* is a how-to manual for climbing out of that rut and rediscovering the creative processes that reside in all of us. It should be on every educator's bookshelf."

—**Sam Wineburg**, Margaret Jacks Professor of Education,
Emeritus, Stanford University and founder of the Stanford History
Education Group

"This is a book for every educator, community member, family member, and policymaker interested in learning more about the work they do to improve it. Drawing from his rich and robust experiences as well as transdisciplinary perspectives on designing and improving teaching, Reich has produced a powerful book that innovates as it educates."

—**H. Richard Milner IV**, Cornelius Vanderbilt Chair of Education; immediate-past president, American Educational Research Association; and author of *The Race Card*

"Intuitively we know that teachers are the driving force of change and administrators need to create the conditions for this to happen, but rarely is that articulated, much less given a road map."

—**Melanie Ching**, director of Community & Engagement at What School Could Be

ITERATE

THE SECRET TO INNOVATION IN SCHOOLS

JUSTIN REICH

JB JOSSEY-BASS™
A Wiley Brand

For general information on our other products and services or for technical support, please contact our Customer Care Department within the United States at (800) 762-2974, outside the United States at (317) 572-3993 or fax (317) 572-4002.

Wiley also publishes its books in a variety of electronic formats. Some content that appears in print may not be available in electronic formats. For more information about Wiley products, visit our web site at www.wiley.com.

Library of Congress Cataloging-in-Publication Data is Available:

ISBN 9781119913504 (Paperback)
ISBN 9781119913528 (ePub)
ISBN 9781119913511 (ePDF)

Cover Design and Illustration: © Haley McDevitt

SKY10052907_080923

To my father, who shared his love of tinkering with me.

CONTENTS

PART III: THE COLLABORATIVE INNOVATION CYCLE

CHAPTER 5: WHAT IS THE COLLABORATIVE INNOVATION CYCLE?

ACKNOWLEDGMENTS

All of the ideas in this book emerge from partnerships over 20 years of teaching and work in schools.

Through the entrepreneurial vision of Tom Daccord, I had the chance to work with schools across the world on implementing new technologies. This work was vital to developing the ideas for the Cycle of Experiment and Peer Learning. With Richard Murnane, John Willett, and Bob Wolf, I led a research project in the 2000s on social media tools in schools, with generous funding from the Hewlett Foundation. That work provided an incredible opportunity to do close observations and interviews with dozens of teachers and schools. My colleagues throughout the years at EdTechTeacher contributed to these ideas with their hard-won insights and through conversations over Tom's many, many birthdays.

The material on the Collaborative Innovation Cycle emerged from a collaboration with Peter Senge at MIT's Sloan School of Management to develop an online course for MITx, *Launching Innovation in Schools*. Elizabeth Huttner was the captain of our online course ship and an invaluable colleague for many years. Elizabeth along with Alyssa Napier and Blake Sims were my co-authors and co-leads for a second MITx course, *Design Thinking for Leading and Learning*. Many of the activities and exercises in this book were developed by them, and nearly all of the materials from our online courses are available (and reused and remixed here) under a Creative Commons license. Microsoft generously funded the development of these courses.

An incredible cadre of educators, some of whom you will meet in this book, generously volunteered their time for interviews and opened their classrooms for my research and courses. All of them, too many to list, have my deepest gratitude for their time and wisdom.

Rachel Slama helped develop and direct the MIT Teaching Systems Lab for five years, and I'm grateful for her leadership that allowed me the time and space to work on this project. The students, staff, and researchers in the TSL have my gratitude for keeping our research on the right track while I've been writing, and I'm especially grateful to my colleagues who read and commented on early drafts of the book. Garrett Beazley makes everything we do look and sound great.

Alyssa Napier has been an incredible thought partner and editor in turning all of this source material into a book, and when I needed a break she spilled all of the tea. Sunnye Collins' developmental edits sharpened the prose throughout the book and spared you from a surfeit of unnecessarily-included adverbs and long subordinate clauses that lengthened many sentences without sufficiently offering all that much additional insight beyond the information provided by the subject and predicate. Amy Fandrei championed this project at Wiley.

I'm always grateful to the ladies in my house for good times and big adventures, but in this case, I am compelled to leave the final thanks to Haley McDevitt, whose incredible illustrations will delight you in the pages ahead.

INTRODUCTION: THE SECRET TO SCHOOL IMPROVEMENT

MY BEST TEACHING EVER: WILDERNESS MEDICINE

I started my education career in an unusual place: I taught wilderness medicine.

During college I worked as an EMT on an ambulance, I taught lifeguarding at the college pool, and I helped run the Blue Ridge Mountain Rescue Group in Virginia. After graduation, I worked for a vocational school in Conway, New Hampshire, called Stonehearth Outdoor Learning Opportunities, or SOLO. They offered multi-day Wilderness First Aid courses to folks working and playing in the outdoors. I taught Navy SEALs, college outdoor program leaders, doctors heading to remote missions across the world, Outward Bound and National Outdoor Leadership School staff, camp counselors, and all kinds of outdoor enthusiasts.

These wilderness medicine classes were incredibly fun to teach, and students loved them. It took me many more years of studying education to understand just how well they were designed. Our students had widely varied education backgrounds—I taught high school graduates alongside practicing physicians—but they all came with a high level of motivation to learn the material: they didn't want to die in the woods! We taught a unit on sprains and fractures: we'd do a lecture on the basic anatomy of bones and muscles and a second lecture on principles of improvising a splint. Then we'd demonstrate how to make a splint out of stuff folks carried in a typical hiking pack, and we'd have people practice inside. Finally, we'd go outside and have a few students pretend to have a broken leg, complete with screams, fake blood, and bruises from stage makeup. The rest of the class would break into groups, assess the scene, treat the injury, and carry the "patients" to safety. Through a combination of direct instruction and practice, students graduated from our short courses with the confidence and know-how to tackle the inevitable misfortunes that happen outdoors.

For two years, I taught this same Wilderness First Aid course over 100 times. Every class had a unit on bone fractures and splinting. I led the lesson myself dozens of times, and I watched my fellow instructors lead the lesson dozens of times as well. Every time I taught the class I would try something just a little different. I'd introduce the topic with a new story. I'd draw a schematic of bone and muscle a little differently. I'd try different materials for demonstrating an improvised splint. I'd tell the same joke that kept folks alert at slightly different points in the lesson sequence. I'd remember the questions that came up at the end of previous lessons and work the answers into a new lecture for the next lesson. I'd tweak the instructions to the students pretending to be patients for the simulations.

After each lesson, I'd reflect on how well I held students' attention, and what questions they asked or didn't. I talked with colleagues about what they observed and how they could do things differently. Perhaps most importantly, during the outdoor training scenarios I walked from group to group and looked at their improvised splints and offered feedback. Right there, on the fake-injured leg of some now-smiling student was the evidence of student learning and my teaching. Was that a splint that would be comfortable? Would it hold a leg straight and stable during a treacherous walk down a wet trail? If one group did something wrong, maybe that was their fault. But if several groups did something wrong, then that was my fault, and I needed to revisit and improve my instruction.

Every lesson was an experiment, and over many iterations my teaching improved. Students would sometimes tell me that I was the best teacher they had ever had. I tried to be gracious, but I knew that these compliments were not the result of any natural gift that I had for teaching. I had one big advantage over all the other teachers I was "competing" against for the best-teacher-in-your-life prize: I had a lot of practice.

If you are an elementary school teacher, at some point during the year you might teach a lesson on how to write a sentence. You might teach that lesson, once per year, in October, and then not again until the following October. If you stay in the classroom for 25 years until you earn your pension, then you will have taught that lesson only 25 times over the course of an entire career.

As a wilderness medicine instructor teaching short courses, it might take me only a few months to teach my splinting lesson 25 times. In a year, I would teach lessons on splinting, tourniquets, or CPR more often than many school teachers would teach any of their lessons over the course of an entire career. As long as I introduced some deliberate experiment, some intentional variation, every time I taught a class, then I could rapidly improve my teaching. I've learned a lot about instruction in the decades since, but those lessons are still probably the best teaching I've done in my life.

CREATING TIME AND SPACE FOR ITERATION

A civics education organization called me recently to discuss their new year-long middle school curriculum, which they were getting ready to pilot. Their plan was to launch the pilot in a few schools in the fall, gather end-of-year data, and refine the course in the summer before a full release the following year. I tried to explain that they might find many of the problems and pain points following that plan but they were severely restricting their opportunities to fix those issues. Teaching is magnificently complex, and excellent instruction requires accounting for prior knowledge, optimal sequencing, engagement, repetition, pacing, analogies, and a zillion other bits of art and science. The plan to pilot this new curriculum left no room for iteration, and instead put all the organization's eggs in a one-year basket.

To be sure, the alternatives I suggested were more complicated. Could they find schools with semester-long courses, where the same teacher could teach the whole class (or key selections) once in the fall and then again in the spring? Could they find student clubs that might run through lessons in advance of the full launch? Could they rearrange the order of some units in schools: maybe one instructor teaches units A/B/C/D, and another teaches B/A/D/C, and after each unit, the teachers get together to share notes to let colleagues build on their learned experience? (Or, even crazier, one teacher leads unit A, the other leads unit B, and then they switch classrooms for the next marking period and teach the same unit again to different students!) But without incorporating more cycles of iteration, the opportunities to find problems, test improvements, and refine new ideas would be much more limited.

In a world where schools increasingly need to respond rapidly to emergencies of all kinds—pandemics, climate-related disasters, political upheavals, refugee movements, and so on—they can no longer afford to have improvement cycles on the scale of one-year courses or five-year strategic plans. However, changing quickly merely for the sake of changing quickly isn't useful either. To improve teaching and learning and to respond effectively to the changing needs of schooling, teachers and school leaders need to develop the ability to experiment, learn from their experiments, and reflect on how to move forward as a team. Teachers need more opportunities to learn, practice, and grow like I did at SOLO, where every time a lesson flopped, I knew I would soon have a chance to try it again.

ITERATIVE IMPROVEMENT AT MIT

Twenty-five years later, I'm now a professor at MIT, where I run a lab called the Teaching Systems Lab. Our mission is to design, implement, and research the future of teacher learning. We teach students on campus and from universities across Boston, we offer online courses across the world, and we create digital clinical simulations where participants can rehearse for and reflect on difficult moments in teaching. I work with a fabulous interdisciplinary team of teacher educators, instructional designers, software developers, post-doctoral researchers, and students of all ages.

One mantra in our lab is that the quality of any product that we offer—an undergraduate class, a grant proposal, a technology platform, an online course, a professional development workshop—usually depends more than anything else on how many cycles of iteration go into the design of that product. If we spend a long time planning, or worse, dithering, and then pull together one draft of something before a deadline, it's rarely great. Our best work occurs when we get a prototype of whatever we are working on in front of people as soon as possible, get feedback, improve the product, and continue this cycle of design, evaluation, and improvement as many times as possible.

One of my favorite ways to express this philosophy comes from Benjamin Erwin's book on teaching with Lego Mindstorms: "Building a robot that works involves building a robot that doesn't work and then figuring out what is wrong with it." To build instruction that works, we first build instruction that doesn't quite work, and then we fix it.[1]

In my time at MIT, I've also had terrific opportunities to collaborate with and learn from computer scientists, entrepreneurs, mechanical engineers, aeronautic experts, and many other folks with unique insights into the art and science of design. They have generously shared their insights with me throughout the years, and I'm excited to pass their wisdom along to you in this book.

THREE CYCLES FOR ITERATIVE IMPROVEMENT

Drawing on my own experiences, my colleagues at MIT, and the incredible work of collaborating educators and designers, this book teaches how to focus on iteration in your work to improve education. With your students, colleagues, families, and other partners, you'll find new ways to bring short cycles of design into the long arc of your teaching year. As you bring this spirit of experimentation to your work, your own teaching will get better faster, and your school community will get better faster, and you'll have more fun doing this important work.

In the pages ahead, I offer three complementary approaches to iterative improvement: the *Cycle of Experiment and Peer Learning*, *Design Thinking for Leading and Learning*, and the *Collaborative Innovation Cycle*. In the spirit of good modeling, this is a book on iteration with three iterative approaches to design and improvement!

Schools are complex systems that operate on multiple levels: individuals, classrooms, and teacher teams (like departments, grade-level teams, or professional learning communities), schools, and districts or networks.

We begin our innovation journey right in the middle, where teachers collaborate and learn from one another. It turns out that this is the most dynamic, exciting, and important space for teacher learning and instructional improvement. As we will see, teacher leadership, sharing, and networking are all indispensable to school improvement. So, the Cycle of Experiment and Peer Learning gets us started right in the mix of this vital work.

The second section of the book zooms into smaller units, like classrooms, libraries, registrar offices, and other places, where individuals and small teams try to improve parts of school. When I was tinkering with my wilderness medicine classes, I was just winging it; trying new things out to make things run more smoothly and keep things interesting for me. But from my colleagues at MIT and educators around the world, I've learned quite a bit about design thinking, a systematic approach to innovation and continuous improvement through cycles of exploration, imagination, prototyping, and testing. Design Thinking for Leading and Learning is one flavor of this approach, developed for teachers and school leaders to be nimble and effective at trying out new approaches to teaching, learning, and living together in schools.

In the third part of the book, we explore the Collaborative Innovation Cycle, and we pan out to examine how bigger entities, like schools and districts, can change and improve together. If the first two cycles of the book provide new tools for individuals and teams to get better faster, this final section of the book will help all those teams coordinate and pull their oars in the same direction.

For each cycle, there are two chapters. The first chapter in each pair is an overview that guides you through the key ideas in each iterative improvement framework, and the second chapter provides hands-on activities for you to try with colleagues. You can read the book from front to back, or you can flip through and look for the approach that seems best aligned with your current challenges. Hopefully, you'll try exercises from all three innovation cycles, and you can discover which one (or ones) work best for you and your colleagues for your particular role and context.

To introduce myself, let me tell you a little bit about the different phases of my career in education, and how I came to study and refine these three iterative approaches to innovation and improvement.

THE CYCLE OF EXPERIMENT AND PEER LEARNING

Part I introduces the Cycle of Experiment and Peer Learning, which describes the processes by which teachers experiment, learn, share, and grow. This model was my answer to a puzzle that plagued me in my first decade working with schools: Why do some schools get better very quickly, and others seem to be more stuck?

I started my classroom teaching career in 2003. When I applied for the job, the department head asked me if I could teach ninth-grade world history. I told him that I never had before, but I promised to study up and be ready to teach the class by Labor Day. Then he told me that their ninth-grade World History class was part of a special technology pilot program, where each classroom had a cart of wireless laptops in the corner of the room. They were blue and orange clamshell MacBooks—an iconic form factor from the early 2000s—and the school had an intranet program called First Class that did most of the things that Google Suite for Education does today from the cloud: messaging, collaborative documents, shared folders, and so forth. He asked if I could teach with these computers each day. I promised him that I could, though honestly, if he had told me there was a cart of

THE CYCLE of EXPERIMENT and PEER LEARNING

bananas in the back corner of the class that I needed to use in class each day, I would have promised him that I could teach with those too. I really needed a job. (Traveling all over the country teaching wilderness medicine is fun, but not great for long-term relationships.)

So, starting in 2003, I wasn't the very first, but I was certainly among the vanguard of US teachers with the opportunity to teach in a 1-to-1 laptop classroom, and I loved it. It was in the early era of the Internet, when museums, governments, and archives were rapidly digitizing their collections, and it was a transformational opportunity for history teachers. When I was a seventh-grade student, my US History class had a primary source reader with 20 documents from the *Mayflower Compact* to the *Letter from a Birmingham Jail*, and that was pretty much it for what we read in class. Fast forward to 2003, and my Internet-connected class had millions and millions of sources that we could access on nearly any topic imaginable.

I had the very good fortune to teach with an entrepreneurial colleague, Tom Daccord, who also taught in the technology-enabled classroom and realized that we were discovering teaching approaches that could benefit many other educators. So, we founded a side-hustle consultancy called EdTechTeacher that worked with schools and districts to integrate technology in service of student-centered learning. In the summers and after I left classroom teaching, I visited schools across the country and around the world, teaching workshops, observing classes, co-teaching lessons, and working with school leadership teams.

Along the way, I enrolled in a doctoral program at the Harvard Graduate School of Education, where I studied how schools adopted new technologies and how those new tools led to instructional improvements. As part of my research, I interviewed dozens of educators and school leaders, and I visited yet more schools—public, private, religious, and charter—in every corner of the country. I found many schools that purchased technology, and few where instruction really seemed to be systematically improving.

Many educators could describe to me the feeling of having new tech seemingly fall from the sky: smartboards that appeared in classrooms or laptop carts that suddenly rolled down hallways. In my hometown of Arlington, Massachusetts, one winter it didn't really snow, and the plowing budget got rolled into tablet computers. It precipitated iPads instead of snow.

Typically, these windfalls came with very little training (and nearly all of it about technical features, not meaningful pedagogy), leadership teams didn't offer much by way of mission or direction ("try it out!"), and teachers didn't receive additional time for planning, collaborating, or otherwise figuring out what to do with the new technology. In a handful of classrooms, teachers came up with some amazing new ideas, but in many places, not much happened. Smartboards became very expensive whiteboards; tablets became expensive notebooks, and school carried on as it had before. This somewhat bleak picture describes most of the schools that I studied and visited, but not all.

The Cycle of Experiment and Peer Learning emerged from trying to describe how teachers learned, changed, and improved in those few schools where new technologies really led to better teaching across departments, grade-level teams, and whole school buildings. In those schools, teachers conducted instructional experiments, reflected on what they learned, and shared their new lessons, strategies, and practices with their colleagues. Teacher-led peer-to-peer learning was the lynchpin of iterative improvement. This posed a bit of a problem for my consultancy and the school leaders who hired us: only people inside classrooms could authentically lead the teaching experiments and the peer-to-peer learning that led to instructional improvement. But over time, I realized that while school leaders couldn't lead this vital process—much like teachers can't really do the learning for their students—they could create the conditions where experimentation and peer-to-peer learning can thrive. So, the Cycle of Experiment and Peer Learning is both a description of how meaningful instructional change actually happens in schools and a prescription for how school leaders can make this process of iterative improvement more efficient, more effective, and more joyful for educators.

DESIGN THINKING FOR LEADING AND LEARNING

After I finished my doctorate, it took me a few twists and turns to find myself as a professor at the Massachusetts Institute of Technology, where we have a small program that lets our undergraduate students (and some wonderful young future educators from Wellesley College) earn a certification to become secondary teachers in math and science. To continue my professional learning work with educators, I started a lab called the Teaching Systems Lab where we aspire to design, implement, and research the future of teacher learning. We work primarily on two problems: creating better online learning for educators and creating more opportunities for teachers to practice.

One bizarre feature of teacher education and teacher in-service learning is that we rarely practice teaching. When teachers learn, they listen to people talk about teaching, and they discuss teaching, but they very rarely *do* teaching. Sometimes teachers have a chance to practice the preparation parts of teaching—designing lesson plans and activities and so forth—but a vital part of teaching is the improvisational interactions between teachers and students. Teachers

DESIGN THINKING

for LEADING and LEARNING

almost never have the chance to practice these crucial interactions. So, a big part of the work in my lab is developing practice spaces: learning environments—inspired by games and simulations—where teachers can rehearse for and reflect on important decisions in teaching. I work with a terrific team of software developers, instructional designers, teacher educators, and measurement experts to build tools that provide the foundation for a more "practiceful" future for teacher education.

MIT is a wonderful place to learn about design. Across the whole university, I'm surrounded by engineers creating new inventions, scientists creating new processes, business school educators creating entrepreneurs, and digital humanists creating the future of the arts. Across our very different disciplines, we have a shared approach to human-centered design: the process of understanding people's real-world challenges and building new tools and practices to help solve those problems. Human-centered design takes place in iterative cycles of discovering, prototyping, testing, refining, and sharing.

In 2014, Microsoft gave my lab a grant to develop online courses for a new platform called MITx, and they asked us to make one of those courses about design thinking in schools. I worked with a talented team of educators to refine everything I had learned about design at MIT into a toolkit that would be useful for K–12 educators: Design Thinking for Leading and Learning. Our approach had two "Ls," leading and learning, because we envisioned two uses for design thinking in schools. First, classroom educators can use design thinking with their students for learning to help them develop the mindset for innovation, design, and change that my colleagues at MIT use every day to invent better futures. Second, educators can turn those same processes inward, and they can use design thinking to lead instructional change and improvement in schools. Design Thinking for Leading and Learning focuses on how teams can design, evaluate, and refine new instructional practices and routines to improve teaching and learning in schools.

There are two chapters in this book that describe the framework of Design Thinking for Leading and Learning and offer practical ideas for putting those ideas to use in your school or context. I also have some additional online resources to help you here. All of the materials from that online course—short documentary videos, explainers, activities, and more—are available at the MIT Open Learning Library (go to openlearninglibrary.mit.edu and search for "Design Thinking for Leading and Learning" or go direct to https://openlearninglibrary. mit.edu/courses/course-v1:MITx+11.155x+1T2019/about). I also have two online "workbooks" that provide complete walkthroughs of design thinking activities: a "starter" exercise about designing a morning routine or party for a friend, and then an exercise for leading school-based learning design. Those workbook chapters are available as free downloads for you and your colleagues at www.wiley.com/go/iterate). For those readers who like a systematic overview of new things, you can read the book chapters first, and for those who like to jump right into the work, you might skip ahead to the activities in those workbooks.

THE COLLABORATIVE INNOVATION CYCLE

The Collaborative Innovation Cycle emerged from my many years of work with school leadership teams. Originally, EdTechTeacher focused on professional learning for teachers, but over time we realized that we could have a more powerful impact on schools if we also worked with school leaders. When Tom Daccord and I worked with schools, he'd run workshops about technology for teacher leaders, and I'd have a meeting with principals, deans, department heads, IT staff, and other administrators.

THE COLLABORATIVE INNOVATION CYCLE

When schools make big investments in curriculum, technology, professional learning, or anything else, there are usually two ways that it can go. Sometimes dictates come down from on high, and teachers are told they need to adapt and change. "We've bought a bunch of computers," say the leaders, "and you all need to figure it out." Those kinds of initiatives often feel like something done to teachers, and they often are not well received. Even when the initiative involves things that could really help, it is very easy for innovation in schools to be perceived by teachers as "just one more thing."

When I worked with school leaders, one of my main tasks was helping them set up new initiatives as something done *with* teachers, rather than *to* them. We'd identify ways to figure out what felt most important and most urgent to rank-and-file faculty, and then plan technology initiatives that were aimed at addressing those pressing challenges. In this framing, the new technology isn't just one more thing to do, but potentially a powerful tool for solving the problems that teachers care most about.

As I will remind you throughout this book, good design is always about balancing tensions. On the one hand, improving schools involves the very granular work of individual teachers trying new practices in their classrooms, and innovation in an advanced high school Mandarin class will look quite different from new reading instruction in a second-grade classroom. However, if every teacher in a school or district pursues their own innovation agenda, the results are too diffuse to benefit everyone. When faculty agree on areas for shared focus, the sum of many classroom experiments is greater than the whole. The Collaborative Innovation Cycle is a set of ideas and practices to help school leaders iteratively guide their communities toward these shared focal areas.

Many of the ideas for the Collaborative Innovation Cycle were developed first for an online course that I taught with Peter Senge called *Launching Innovation in Schools*. The free courseware for that course is also available at the MIT Open Learning Library. You can go to openlearninglibrary.mit.edu and search for "Launching Innovation in Schools" or https://openlearninglibrary.mit.edu/courses/course-v1:MITx+11.154x+3T2018/about.

THREE PRINCIPLES FOR ITERATION

In our work together in the pages ahead, I ask you to make three big shifts in your thinking about how you can make teaching and learning better in your school, college, or workplace.

THINK IN CYCLES AND SPIRALS

First, when we imagine the future of our work, think about cycles and spirals instead of straight lines and linear narratives. School boards have five-year strategic plans with beginnings, middles, and ends; teachers have pacing guides that go from September to June. Linear narratives shape all kinds of thinking in education, and we will reimagine those straight lines as spirals of improvement, with many iterative cycles of launching, evaluation, and tinkering. When we approach problems with linear thinking, we put finding problems

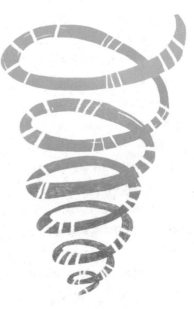

at the beginning, developing solutions in the middle, and evaluation at the end. But often, we learn from developing solutions and evaluating them that we misunderstood the real problems when we started. Spirals of improvement let us regularly return to the framing of our problems as we design and test new solutions.

ACT IN SHORT DESIGN CYCLES

Second, let's make those design cycles as short as we can. The arc of school is so long: units take weeks, classes take months, schools take years, the system spans over 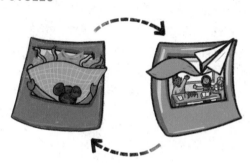 a decade. It's incredibly hard to get better at something if you try it once in September and you don't get another shot at it until the next September. In one of our Teaching Systems Lab workshops, a novice teacher once said to us, "I used to think about whether I had a good lesson, now I'm thinking about whether I had a good minute of teaching." Let's bring a bias to action to our work, and find more places in our educational work where we can try small things more quickly.

IMPROVE IN COMMUNITY

Third, let's invite lots of people to join those design cycles with us. School buildings are so strange in that we build walls such that each adult is in their own room alone. Learning alone is hard!

Improving alone is hard! Instead of imagining the improvement of teaching as the solitary quest of individuals, think of improved teaching as a community endeavor. Students, colleagues, family members, and communities can all be involved in helping us implement short spirals of design, evaluation, and improvement. Be particularly attentive to how marginalized folks in our communities—families who have recently arrived in the United States, students who experience discrimination, folks who think and learn differently—can be powerful allies in creating better learning environments.

Lines to spirals, long schools to short cycles, individual improvement to community partnerships. When you figure out how to make iteration central to your teaching, you'll improve faster, your community will benefit from your improvements, and you'll find that teaching is more fun and more energizing. Hopefully, you'll become someone's best teacher ever. Let's get started.

A note on illustrations: All of the beautiful images, comics, and illustrations in this book are available for reuse and remixing under a Creative Commons CC:BY license, which means you can use them if you attribute them to the brilliant illustrator Haley McDevitt. We're hoping that as you finish the book, you'll decide to share what you've learned with your colleagues and students. If you develop slides, worksheets, or other resources for sharing and teaching, feel free to use the images, which you can find in a folder at haleymcdevitt.com/iterate.

THE CYCLE OF EXPERIMENT
AND PEER LEARNING

WHAT IS THE CYCLE OF EXPERIMENT AND PEER LEARNING?

If you want to improve teaching and learning in schools, you should start by understanding how schools change. Once you understand the catalysts that inspire teachers to change their practice, it's much easier to plan ways of leading innovation and launching new ideas.

This is a book about planning and facilitating iterative change, and the good news is that school change is already cyclical. Even if you think that schools get better through five-year strategic plans, if you zoom down into classrooms, departments, and grade-level teams, you will find that improvements are shaped by cycles rather than stages, by spirals of improvement rather than the unfolding of annual plans.

I've spent the better part of the past 20 years investigating how new education technologies impact schools. All too often, the sad answer is: not much. Schools around the country and across the world have made major investments in broadband, laptops, tablets, and other technologies in the hopes of improving student learning. In most places, even widespread adoption of new technology tools doesn't lead to changes in teaching practice that substantially improve student learning.[1]

I remember visiting one of the very first high schools in the United States to have one computing device for every student, in this case an Apple iPad. I asked students what their favorite application was for the tablets. The overwhelming answer was a note-taking app: Evernote. They really liked taking notes for all their classes on one device, rather than in separate notebooks. That was their sense of the main change in their education! Spending $800 per student to consolidate notebooks is not the best return on a community investment.

I've taught classes about education and online learning at MIT for a decade, and I often start class by asking students to tell me their "edtech story," something distinctive about new technologies from their own school experience. For the past few years, I've found myself in the "smartboard generation." My students are usually 19 or 20 years old, and when they were in middle school, digital whiteboards started appearing in their classrooms. Almost universally, students tell me that the digital features of these tools went entirely unused; they were just whiteboards. Sometimes students say the whiteboards got pushed to the side or the back of the classroom.

Out of all the schools I've visited, I have only been to a few places where new technologies really lead to new patterns in teaching and learning. Usually, really exciting changes are just limited to a pocket of a school or community. I visited a seventh-grade team in rural New Hampshire that reorganized all their classes for a few weeks—science, ELA, social studies, specials—around a giant collaborative history investigation that resulted in a collaborative website. It was a terrific initiative that defined learning for students for the whole year. But while this digital project was a highlight of the seventh-grade experience, not much seemed to have changed in the other grades.

While I was working on my dissertation, shortly after Google Docs was released for schools, I visited a middle school in southern California where iterative writing practices—with more frequent drafts, peer review, and teacher feedback—had spread across multiple courses and grades.[2] Students and teachers could describe concrete ways that writing instruction across the subjects had changed—and how student writing had improved—because of new schoolwide technology practices using Google Docs.

Whenever I encounter these places where change seems to have moved forward with striking breadth and depth, I always try to understand the details of how that change happened. I have visited and consulted with a zillion schools where new devices fall like a stone in a lake—a big splash, a few ripples, and then the lake returns to its former balance. How did this one school manage to make a substantial, important change in how they helped students learn, not just in a classroom or two, but in many classrooms throughout the building?

I asked some of the teachers about the role of school leadership, and the mystery only deepened. "I'm not sure they know exactly what we are doing," one told me. What?!? I'm in a school where it really seems like some interesting changes are happening, and the principal team is just happily hiring subs and making sure the buses run on time? The faculty described a kind of benign neglect of school leadership regarding these teaching changes: they were fine with it, the results seemed good, but they weren't really helping the process along, beyond letting teachers lead the way.

This story doesn't make any sense if you have a vision of change where strong leadership comes in with a clear direction, tells people how to improve teaching and learning, and then supports them in implementing new techniques and strategies. How can teaching change under the benign neglect of formal leadership? To expand the puzzle a bit: What is different about the schools where improvements are widespread and systemic, compared to places where changes seem more isolated and slow? To explain, you need a theory of teaching improvement and innovation where change can emerge from the bottom up in classrooms, libraries, and learning spaces.

CHANGING THE COMPLEX, FINE-GRAINED WORK OF TEACHING

If you want to understand the California school that lifted their writing instruction with collaborative writing tools, or if you want to understand any school where meaningful change in teaching is happening, then you have to recognize two crucial, underlying features of schools that dictate how nearly any kind of improvement unfolds.

First, schools are unfathomably complicated, and the classroom work of teaching is very, very fine grained. Think about a typical PK–12 school district in America, and everything that's happening in it today. A kindergartener is learning to tie her shoes or stand in line. A third-grader is using manipulatives to try to get a conceptual handle on fractions. A fifth-grader with Down syndrome is getting occupational therapy. A seventh-grader is starting a new unit on sex education. There are students conjugating Spanish verbs, factoring polynomials, reflecting on the book *Beloved*, fixing cars, saying the Pledge of Allegiance, learning to critique their government, and on and on and on. It's baffling and magical that one institution can do all those things for all those different children.

When I say the work of teaching is fine grained, I mean that much of what happens in a kindergarten classroom is just not that relevant to the work in a calculus class. If you make a teaching unit better in Earth Science, it's not really going to help the Phys Ed teacher all that much. In fact, if you improve a plate tectonics unit in Earth Science, it may not even help your meteorology unit. Even within the same classroom, what we do from day to day and week to week can be startlingly different. We can certainly learn from one another, but implementing teaching improvements is often extremely local and anchored to one classroom.

That fine-grained complexity is why it's so hard for big, whole-school teaching initiatives to work. Let's say you are a superintendent, fresh out of your Doctorate in Education program, and you think that teaching should be data-driven, so you focus on formative assessment for the first few years. There are 13 grades of schooling in the district, dozens of courses across the subject areas, and 40 or so weeks of school. If you want one formative assessment a week in all those subjects in all those grand bands, you've just placed an order for thousands of new formative assessments, many of which will be quite different in important ways; the formative assessments about irony in *Romeo and Juliet* will be quite different from the formative assessments about state capitals.

Importantly, there are not enough administrators in your district office or your school building to do all this design work and to implement it in classrooms. The only people who can change teaching and learning in schools are classroom teachers—and library-media specialists, and aides, and paraprofessionals, and all the amazing people who work directly with youth. That's the punch line of this meditation on the fine-grained complexity of schools: ***the only people who can actually change teaching and learning in schools are classroom teachers.***

Teachers are the only professionals who are numerous enough in school buildings to implement new teaching practices, all of which need to be customized to the specific needs of the particular subjects, topics, and students in a given classroom. For the school leaders reading: you can certainly help, and I'll get to that, but it's worth starting with some humility about what you can accomplish. You personally are not going to order changes or demonstrate some effective technique that will be rapidly cloned by your faculty. All change has to be localized classroom by classroom by teachers.

TEACHERS PRIMARILY CHANGE THEIR PEDAGOGY IN RESPONSE TO OTHER TEACHERS

So, if teachers are the only people who can implement teaching changes, then we arrive at the essential question of school improvement: *How do teachers learn to adopt new changes?* A very straightforward way to answer this vital question is just to ask teachers, like my colleague John Diamond did in Chicago public schools during the No Child Left Behind era. Professor Diamond asked teachers to describe who influenced what they taught—their curriculum—and who influenced how they taught—their pedagogy. There was a mix of answers to the question of who influences curriculum: school leaders, state standards, and so forth. But to the question of who influences teaching practice, one answer stood out above all others: *other teachers*.[3]

Teachers primarily change their practice in response to other teachers. With great apologies to principals, superintendents, educational consultants, coaches, publishers, and all the other people who are trying to contribute to this work, you are all second fiddlers (myself included!). The person most likely to influence a teacher's practice is their colleague.[4]

If you start from this bedrock fact that teachers primarily change their practice in response to inspiration and guidance from other teachers, then the whole work of school improvement centers around peer learning. School leadership can be tremendously important, but it's not what directly changes classroom practice. For school leaders, if you want teaching to change, then your primary job is to create conditions where teachers can learn from one another. Teacher leadership is urgent and vital. Classroom teachers, if school change is going to happen, it will come from you! In fact, it can *only* come from you.

As I've watched groups of teachers, grade-level teams, departments, and whole schools work on teaching improvements over the years, I've come to describe this work as the *Cycle of Experiment and Peer Learning*. In my research, I used the Cycle of Experiment and Peer Learning to explain the places where technology didn't sink like a stone, but, rather, led to meaningful changes in teaching practice. Since that work, I've come to realize that almost any story of school improvement has features of this cycle, because teacher innovation and leadership is at the center of the Cycle of Experiment and Peer Learning, and at the center of any real teaching changes in schools.

THE CYCLE of EXPERIMENT and PEER LEARNING

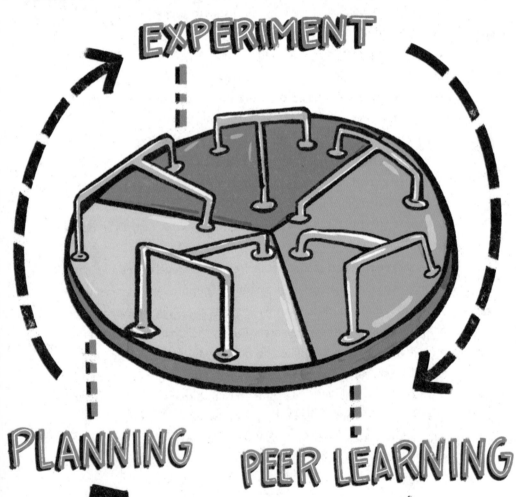

EXPERIMENT

PLANNING

PEER LEARNING

THREE PHASES TO THE CYCLE
OF EXPERIMENT AND PEER LEARNING

The Cycle of Experiment and Peer Learning has three parts: Experiment, Peer Learning, and Planning. Experimentation is when one teacher or a small group of educators tries out something new in a classroom, library, gym, or other learning space. Peer learning flows naturally from experiments, as educators discuss what they've tried and reflect on how it went. When experiments go well, more people get excited about them and want to get involved. Planning is the process of bringing people together to refine existing experiments and launch new ones. Here's how the whole cycle works:

EXPERIMENT

In many classrooms, teaching is in a steady state, an equilibrium. As teachers, we fumble our way to syllabi, curricula, units, routines, and methods that work, and most teachers tend to stick with the tried and true on most days. There are lots of reasons for this equilibrium. One of the main ones is time: compared to other affluent countries around the world, teachers in the United States spend more time directly with students and less time on planning and collaboration than peers in other comparable countries. If you don't have time to plan and collaborate, it's hard to do new things.[5]

And let's be honest, trying new things in teaching is scary. It's embarrassing when a new lesson or new teaching technique flops. It's incredibly frustrating when you try a new technology and the logins don't work, or the Internet is slow, or it all just takes too long. Teachers know about how long their typical methods will take, but it's hard to predict how much time new approaches will consume from a lesson or a week. Many long-time teachers also suffer from "initiative fatigue." Every few years, they get a new principal or superintendent, who comes into the role hoping to promote their favored approach or innovation. States and communities make all kinds of demands of schools: new emphases, new concerns, new regulations. In many schools, these efforts tend to come and go, and teachers learn that it can be easier to sit on the sidelines and wait them out, rather than really diving into every new fad or idea that comes along.

But in every school I've visited, there's always a group of teachers willing to chart out into the unknown. They're willing to stay up late planning, toss out old lesson plans, and try something new. They thrive in exploration, experimentation, and uncertainty. And they can appear anywhere in a school: in the third grade, in the history department, among a few close friends with the tech director. There is a stereotype that the teachers most willing to experiment are young and new to the profession—and certainly those late planning nights are easier without young kids at home. But I've also found that there are lots of veteran classroom teachers who are masters of their craft, and they enjoy tweaking and improving. They have so many robust systems and routines set up that they have the time to be deliberate about trying new things. Kate Lewis, a veteran middle school teacher in Massachusetts, described the joys and trials of innovation this way:

Experimenting is exciting because the students are doing something new and you're doing something new, so they pick up on your enthusiasm for a new project or a new topic. It can be challenging, because sometimes things don't quite work out the way you expect them to. For example, my students were working on a collaborative book that we were going to all make together about grammar. However, once it got down to the logistical pieces of putting it all together, it just kind of fell apart. So sometimes you try something, and it doesn't work, and you just have to say, all right, what am I going to do moving forward to improve this? How could I make this better? But it's exciting when you see the kids get a spark, and they get excited about it, and they love doing the project.

PEER LEARNING

When teachers like Kate Lewis try new projects in their classroom, usually the work happens with at least a few other people. I saw this frequently with teachers experimenting with new technology projects. The projects required students to do some research, so the teacher connected with the librarian. The project used a new technology tool, so the technology staff got involved. There was an aide or a paraprofessional in the classroom helping. In some cases, a few teachers worked together on the project. Sometimes a student would wander into class, look at you askance, and say, "Hey, how come we're not doing what Ms. Lewis's class is doing?" And then you grin and respond, "Because Ms. Lewis loves her students more than I do," and then you go catch up with Ms. Lewis about what it is that she was up to.

Through these collaborations and encounters, usually a few teachers have a chance to discuss and reflect on a new initiative. Ms. Lewis asks, "What am I going to do moving forward to improve this?" and teachers look at the students' work to search for evidence of deep learning. They ask students what they liked and didn't like about the new lesson. They get some feedback from the aide helping some of their special education students. Through these conversations and reflection, teachers involved in the project come to understand what worked, what didn't, and how to improve. Educators at the periphery of the innovation get interested in hearing about it and consider trying new things.

Most schools are pretty good about having formal and informal spaces where these conversations can happen. Here's Kate Lewis again, talking about where these spaces are in her middle school in central Massachusetts:

> *In the middle school level, we teach as part of a team. So, we meet daily with the science, social studies, math, and language arts teachers, every single day. And that's a great time to just shoot out, "Hey, guess what I did, and this worked great." And then the other teachers think of ways that they can do similar things in their own classrooms, in their subjects. And then it helps spread it . . . . Also, we have biweekly curriculum meetings. So, every other week, each department meets together. And that's a really great time to share things that worked and to get feedback on it. We also have professional development days, where we're able to bring things in to our colleagues to get their feedback and ideas for improvement.*

> *For example, this Friday, I'm in the process of developing a really big project-based learning unit with the math teacher on my team, and it focuses on starting a business, but more than that. It's about "What does it take to be successful in the world?" And I'm going to take it to my colleagues on Friday to do a project tuning protocol. So, I'll just bring it, and I will tell them "Here's what I'm really struggling with. What are your ideas? What can you do? What do you see here as the strengths and weaknesses?" And you kind of have to be willing to put things out there for everyone, even though they may have some critiques, but that's okay, because you need to take the critiques and learn from them.*

When Chicago teachers in Professor Diamond's research said they primarily change their practice in response to other teachers, it's these kinds of formal and informal interactions that they are often talking about. In professional learning communities, grade-level teams, department meetings, teachers' lounges, and increasingly on social media, teachers hear about new things that are interesting, engaging, and help support student learning, and they talk about them with their colleagues. These reflections both help innovators refine their practice and draw more teachers into trying these experiments.

My MIT colleague Peter Senge has worked for many years with schools on systems change, and he describes most teachers as "patient pragmatists." In general, schools only have a few folks who are die-hard, constant experimenters. On the other end of the spectrum, schools typically only have a few teachers who are truly resistant to change. (And those who are resistant to change are usually not opposed to improvements; they are just skeptical that changes lead to improvements.) Most teachers are sitting on the proverbial fence, waiting for someone else to give something a try, waiting for some evidence that a new teaching idea has some legs and is likely to be fun, engaging, and effective for learning before they hop off the fence and jump in. I don't mean that as a criticism: a school where every teacher was constantly trying new things would be chaotic and exhausting. Descriptively, most new improvement efforts in schools are not taken up widely at first; if a few innovators make some progress, then others will prove willing to hop in and join along.[6]

PLANNING

That leads to the third step of the Cycle of Experiment and Peer Learning: planning. When teachers try something new, they discover things that work and fail; they tinker and revise. If something seems pretty good, a teacher will tell a few colleagues, and a

few folks will hop off the fence and join. Separately or together, they'll plan a new iteration of the change initiative, this time with some more people, some bigger efforts, some deeper changes to plans, routines, or techniques. Again, Kate Lewis has sound advice for how planning starts to scale up change:

> *Start small but don't stay small. Make one small change. Maybe you have a project you've been doing for years that could use a little refreshment. Refresh that project. Just do one thing. And then next year, maybe try changing something new. And then eventually, what ends up happening is you're just changing everything. It's like, start small, but then get bigger as you go.*

Ms. Lewis recognizes that improvements in teaching are almost always inherently iterative. You start small and get bigger as you repeat, revisit, and expand your experiments. When you visit the schools where teaching and learning are constantly improving bit by bit, you'll see teachers at all stages of this cycle: launching experiments, reflecting with colleagues, planning new experiments.

In observing these cycles in many schools, one charitable way to describe these activities is that they have a kind of natural, intuitive quality. Individual teachers are out there picking and choosing new things to try and refining their work here and there. But another way to describe this process is that teachers are planting a thousand flowers to bloom without any overall strategy. Teacher experimentation is often not part of any broader, coherent plan for school improvement. And teachers are often not very systematic about how they plan new experiments—about how they solicit student input, prototype, and evaluate new ideas, or test their innovation efforts. In the second and third sections of *Iterate*, I offer you more structured tools for thinking through and conducting this kind of work. In Part II, Design Thinking for Leading and Learning, we'll work through a protocol for designing new teaching ideas that helps you systematically evaluate challenges, design prototypes, and test new solutions. In Part III, the Collaborative Innovation Cycle, we explore another innovation cycle that focuses on bringing coherence to these diverse efforts, so that lots of diverse experiments reinforce collaborative learning rather than simply diverging in a thousand directions.

WHAT'S MISSING FROM THE CYCLE OF EXPERIMENT AND PEER LEARNING

The Cycle of Experiment and Peer Learning is the result of *descriptive research*. When I was forming these ideas in my early research, I wasn't trying to make an argument about what *should* be happening, I was trying to describe what I saw. Maybe not surprisingly, what happens typically and naturally in schools isn't necessarily the best possible path forward. After reflecting over the past 15 years, I think there are three important ideas whose absence in the Cycle of Experiment and Peer Learning is worth noting.

EVALUATION AND MEASUREMENT

What does it mean when a teacher says "a lesson worked better" or "an activity didn't work"? While executing a lesson—asking questions, guiding activities, giving lectures, responding to student  queries—teachers are also trying to figure out if a lesson is going well. Like many things in education, this evaluation is deceptively difficult to do. First off, if you are trying something new in your classroom, it probably takes a substantial amount of your concentration and attention just to make the procedures of the lesson work. What did I plan to say here? How many minutes should this part take? If you are thinking about these questions while you are trying something new, it's also hard to be scanning the room and looking for evidence as to whether your teaching is working.

Even if you could concentrate on your teaching and 27 kids' learning at the same time, it's quite difficult to casually diagnose whether a lesson is working. A complete disaster is obvious: students can't follow directions, complete activities, or actively describe their confusion. But when things at least sort of work, it's very difficult to tell what kinds of learning experiences students had. If they follow instructions and complete activities, is that because the instructions were too rote, and they don't understand the underlying concepts? If they claim that a learning experience was confusing or difficult, does that represent a good amount of desirable difficulty? If they claim a learning experience was enjoyable and clear, does that mean that the teacher did too much of the heavy lifting and hard thinking? Can students transfer what they've learned from one lesson to the next lesson? The next unit? Another domain?

My colleague Ilana Horn argues that when teachers quickly or intuitively evaluate their own teaching, one of the main characteristics they look for is "smoothness." Were students compliant and generally happy? Did they ask some questions but not too many? Did they generally complete the planned tasks? Smoothness has its place in an orderly school or classroom, but smoothness does not ensure learning. Friction can be a great indicator of interesting learning. Smoothness can be a better signal of compliance than of insight.[7]

Answering questions about student learning and experience requires attention to measurement and evaluation. In my observations of schools and in my interviews and discussions with educators, I didn't see or hear much about systematic approaches to evaluating new approaches to teaching. A better version of the Cycle of Experiment and Peer Learning might be Experiment – Peer Learning – Evaluate – Plan. A core part of the Design Thinking for Leading and

Learning cycle is testing hypotheses and gathering evidence to confirm or reject them. A major part of the Collaborative Innovation Cycle is measuring progress and adjusting. So, in future chapters, I'll say more about evaluation, but I want to note here that it's an important piece of good iterative improvement that's often not an intuitive part of how educators experiment.

LOSS

I work in school innovation because I think it's really fun. When a new instructional technique sparks student interest, and when teachers can see how iterative improvements lead to rich, deeper student learning, that's incred-

ibly exciting to me. When a group of educators pull together to build new things that are better than what they have been doing before, and when the work of that improvement feels collaborative and joyful, I find those spaces energizing.

But change is also inherently bound up with loss. That loss is obvious with changes that move schools in the wrong direction. Many early childhood educators have critiqued the push toward making early grades like kindergarten more academic and more structured, and they mourn the loss of time devoted to play, exploration, and spontaneity in those grades.[8]

It's easy to observe that kind of loss when schools change for the worse, but that loss is also found even with efforts to improve teaching and learning. One of my earliest school improvement efforts was as a ninth-grade world history teacher. I was part of a four-person team that taught *History of the Human Community*, a world history class that covered early hominids through the Renaissance. It was a kind of death march history class, the Sumarians on Monday, Mesopotamia on Tuesday, and on and on, plowing through the empires until you made it to the Medicis in Florence. At the end of my second year, my colleagues and I realized that nobody really liked this class. The students, even those who loved history, rarely rated it their favorite class. We didn't really like teaching it. We were basically still offering the course because some long-retired guy had created it years ago, and we just stuck with it.

We decided to reformat the course as four major units, where in each unit we'd trace the identities of people involved in contemporary conflicts back into the ancient world. We covered many fewer topics and periods in history, but we taught our carefully selected topics with much greater depth.[9]

Generally, my fellow world history teachers were supportive of this plan, but the changes were quite hard for my dear colleague Tom Daccord. Tom had developed two fantastic units about the Greek and Roman empires. There were good reasons to leave these out of the new curriculum: most of our students had experience with them in middle school, and we had a good classics department that afforded opportunities for interested students to pursue more advanced study. But Tom loved those units, had poured his heart into them, and he was really, genuinely sad to see them cut from the curriculum.

The story has a happy ending. Tom eventually, with some reluctance, agreed to our changes, we all taught the new course together, and it went brilliantly. With the benefit of hindsight, Tom agreed with our assessment that the benefits of a narrower, deeper curriculum were worth the costs of sidelining some of his favorite content to teach. He became a great advocate for our work within and beyond the school.

But—and here's the important part—*it still hurt*. Even though we were incredibly excited to be doing something new, and we needed the energy from that excitement to power us through all the extra work a curriculum reform requires, we still needed to make space for Tom's sadness. Our change necessitated that Tom lose something he cared about. It wasn't just a pair of well-planned units. Teaching about the Greeks and Romans was part of Tom's identity as a teacher and as a citizen.

Usually when I talk and write about the Cycle of Experiment and Peer Learning, I describe teachers like Kate Lewis who are having a ball with their students trying new things. But it's also important to recognize the sadness and loss inherent in change—not just inherent in people resisting changes they don't like, but in adjusting to changes that they ultimately believe in. People need to mourn loss; at the time, I'm not sure we did enough to help Tom have a little space to say goodbye to his work with the Greeks and Romans.

Since change involves loss, it also inevitably involves addressing people's emotions, managing conflict and disagreement, and bringing a sense of empathy to the work. My MIT colleague Peter Senge sometimes says that we too often mistake leadership as a "neck-up" activity, all brains and no heart. In the Collaborative Innovation Cycle in Part III, I explicitly adjust how we can "manage the ups and downs" of the change process. But for now, it's enough to say that even though the Cycle of Experiment and Peer Learning is about iterating toward something better, and the process overall can be quite joyful and satisfying, we know that some people involved will experience loss along the way.

POWER, DIFFERENCE, AND DESIGN JUSTICE

In researching school change and technology adoption, I was often asking the question "How do learners from different backgrounds and life circumstances use technology differently?" For instance, when I observed and interviewed teachers experimenting with new technology-rich approaches to teach- ing and learning, they would first try new things with their Advanced Placement classes or with their Honors students. Stu-  dents in regular classes missed out.

Teachers had sensible reasons for making these decisions: advanced classes were smaller, their students were more resil- ient to teaching failures, they had fewer issues with disruptive stu- dent behavior, and so forth. In some cases, teachers piloted cool new things with their AP students that they then used with all their classes. But in some cases, teachers focused their innovation efforts on their students in advanced classes, and the benefits were limited to those groups. The opportunities to be in advanced classes are not distributed equally. Black, Latino, and Native American students are less likely to have the opportunity to be in these classes than White students; affluent students are more likely to be in these classes than working-class students.[10]

So, when the teachers that I observed focused their innova- tion efforts on the most advanced students, they were also often focusing their extra planning and improvement time on the most well-supported, already-successful students under their care. These classroom-level patterns that I saw in my observations also cohered with findings from national surveys of teachers and students. For dec- ades, researchers have studied technology use in school and found consistently that when young people use technology in schools, White and affluent students are more likely to use edtech for creative expression or complex projects with substantial adult mentorship and support, while poverty-impacted students and students from minority backgrounds are more likely to use technology for drill-and-practice applications with less support from adults and mentors. What seemed to teachers like a sensible, defensible local choice was contributing to broad national patterns that I believe most educators would find unacceptable. It is possible to innovate in ways that reduce inequalities, but it is also quite possible to innovate in ways that reinforce existing inequalities.[11]

Iteration is a tool, and potentially a powerful one. We do not all have equal power and standing to take risks. A tenured teacher can take different stances toward innovation than a pre-tenure teacher can. My LGBTQ colleagues and colleagues from racial, ethnic, and religious minority groups bear risks in their innovation work that are different from the risks that I take on as an affluent White guy. Power and difference not only affect the outcomes of our improvement efforts, but also people's experiences within those improvement efforts.

The Cycle of Experiment and Peer Learning doesn't attend to these kinds of issues of power, difference, and opportunity. It describes an iterative improvement process, but it doesn't offer any guidance to direct that process toward aims that heal divisions, reduce systematic inequalities, or necessarily promote positive change. None of the three frameworks presented in this book have an explicit step that asks you, in your improvement effort, to stop and have an "equity moment" or go through a "justice evaluation process." Instead, at every step of our iterative improvement efforts, we need to ask who is in the room, how people are being included, and how power and difference shape our goals.

Every model simplifies reality so we can make sense of it, and the Cycle of Experiment and Peer Learning is no exception. I have highlighted evaluation, loss, and power as three dimensions that seem conspicuously absent to me; other missing pieces might be obvious to you. The point, as with thinking about putting this model into action, is to give us something simple enough to start with and communicate to others, while recognizing that the immense complexity of schools in a diverse, democratic society means that we will always have to build nuance into our thinking. I hope you'll keep these missing pieces in mind, as we turn toward putting the Cycle of Experiment and Peer Learning to work!

LEADERSHIP AND THE CYCLE OF EXPERIMENT AND PEER LEARNING

Now that we have a model for how teaching changes—teacher to teacher, one at a time—in classrooms, we can go back to our puzzling question from the beginning of this chapter: What is different about the schools in which improvements are widespread and systemic, compared to places where changes seem isolated and slow?

In schools with systemic, widespread change, teachers try new practices, debrief those experiences with colleagues, and share what they've learned with others. As other teachers learn about new innovations, they move beyond individual classrooms across departments, grades, and entire schools. The Cycle of Experiment and Peer Learning describes this process of learning, sharing, and iterative improvement.

The good news is that every school has educators participating in the Cycle of Experiment and Peer Learning. I've never visited a school that didn't have these seeds planted somewhere. But a few things distinguish the schools where improvements are happening more widely and readily. First, the Cycle of Experiment and Peer Learning is spinning faster: there are more experiments, more reflections, and more plans happening. A major point of emphasis throughout this book is that the structure of curriculum—three-week units, four-month semesters, nine-month academic years—can make iteration unfold over years. But as teachers, we don't have that many years in our whole careers! So, if we want iteration to lead to deeper, wider change, we have to find ways to spin the cycle faster. Second, we need these cycles to constantly draw in more people. When Ms. Lewis talks about starting small and getting bigger as you go, she's talking about making pedagogical changes that deepen with each passing cycle in an individual classroom. But we also want our best ideas and most productive changes spreading across multiple classrooms.

That was what was so special about what was happening in the Southern California school that had embraced iterative, collaborative writing across the curriculum. They weren't just making teaching better in one classroom, they were sharing ideas and routines with each other so that the practices could be shared across different subjects and grade levels. And they did it without any designated school-wide collaborative writing or Google Docs initiative, and indeed without even having much engagement from school leadership at all. That's perhaps not the best way for change to happen, but it is a powerful demonstration for how teacher leadership, teacher innovation, and teacher peer-to-peer learning is essential to the Cycle of Experiment and Peer Learning, and how teaching and learning improves in classrooms.

The bottom-up, teacher-led, Cycle of Experiment and Peer Learning often is the real driver of change even when an initiative appears to be top-down and imposed by some administration. If you peer closely enough into nearly any teaching effort at schools—new curriculum, new technology, new teaching approaches—you'll find that it is exceedingly rare that a principal gets up at a faculty meeting and says, "Now, we're all doing it this way," and all of the faculty leap out of their seats and say, "Yes, definitely; that's a great way; let's do that!"

Schools are what sociologists call "loosely coupled" institutions: there is visible hierarchy, but the many folks at the bottom of the hierarchy do not reliably follow directives from the top. Aviation is a tightly coupled industry. If the FAA requires some additional maintenance check or preflight step, it will happen quickly and universally. (Think of how fast the technologies, policies, and practices of mobile phones and "airplane mode" spread across the entire global aviation industry.) School is not like that.[12]

A school can mandate a new textbook for the math department, but many teachers will still use their old slides, worksheets, and activities for the first few years. Someone in the department will try out the new program in a full-bore, whole-hog way, and report to colleagues on how it's going. Teachers will discuss what works particularly well in the new textbook, what materials from older systems are still superior, and slowly a group of faculty might over time migrate to a new program. Even when change looks like it results from decisions made by school leadership, the actual adoption on the ground is slower, more collaborative, and more iterative.

Once you understand how the Cycle of Experiment and Peer Learning works in schools, the role of leadership in schools becomes clearer.

First and foremost, teacher leadership is essential to starting, scaling, and sustaining new practices in schools. You can't have new practices without teachers and librarians and other instructional folks putting those practices in action, and you can't spread those practices without teachers sharing and teaching one another. There are not enough administrators in any school building or district to do all the incredibly fine-grained, lesson-by-lesson, unit-by-unit, subject-by-subject design and redesign that innovation requires. And even if the school principal is highly regarded as a master teacher, current practicing teachers are less interested in getting their pedagogical tips from someone out of the classroom. They want to learn and grow with their peers who are currently teaching. If you are a teacher, your leadership in service of change and innovation in schools is indispensable.

Now, if you are a principal, or a school consultant, or an MIT professor who hasn't taught in a K–12 classroom in 15 years, then it's important to bring humility to your leadership work. People outside the classroom cannot do the most important work that pedagogical innovation requires, which is inventing and refining new practices and sharing them with others. Instead, your role is providing the time, resources, encouragement, and support to grease the gears of this cycle. Your job is to empower teachers so that they can conduct experiments, share and learn with colleagues, and then plan further experiments. Ideally, you can help this cycle spin faster, and with more opportunities for joy, reflection, and camaraderie. Teachers, sadly, are rarely paid extra for refining their teaching instead of sticking with what they've always done. In places where educators are constantly working to refine their practice, they often do so because they see how it benefits students, and because they simply enjoy experimentation and collaboration with colleagues. Making these efforts enjoyable is an essential part of making them sustainable. In the next chapter, we explore how we can support teachers in these important activities.

Sell your books at
sellbackyourBook.com!
Go to sellbackyourBook.com
and get an instant price
quote. We even pay the
shipping - see what your old
books are worth today!

00058927563

0005892

7563 L

Ms. Mills wondered how to get all her students engaged in their current topic -- even the quiet ones...

SOCRATIC SEMINAR

She decided to introduce her class to Socratic seminars as an experiment.

Afterwards, at lunch with colleagues, Ms. Mills shared how well the Socratic seminar went.

Look what I brought!

Oh yum! Is that your newest recipe?

Wait, I have to tell you both all about how class went first!

Her department head, Mr. Davis, visited the class and encouraged others to do the same.

Thank you for subbing in for me! I'll be back in twenty.

You're welcome! Enjoy visiting Ms. Mill's class!

The principal was thrilled to see the English department rally around a new idea that engaged students.

FUNDING for 3 EXTRA PEOPLE to ATTEND the STATE ENGLISH TEACHERS CONFERENCE

We look forward to your support as a coach next year!

I'm honored!

Ms. Mills was granted a one-course release to help other teachers prepare their Socratic seminars, which Mr. Davis said everyone should try at least once this fall.

SPINNING THE CYCLE OF EXPERIMENT AND PEER LEARNING

If you grew up in the 1980s, as I did, there is a good chance your playground had a merry-go-round. These weren't big carousels with horses and motors and such, but a circular metal platform mounted so that it could spin freely. Kids hung onto metal rods that extended up from the platform as the merry-go-round spun faster and faster. Those same rods also let people standing on the ground push on the rods to make the merry-go-round go round and round.

RESEARCH AND DEVELOPMENT

- ☐ TOOLS
- ☐ RESOURCES
- ☐ EXPERTISE
- ☐ TIME

TEAM LEARNING

OPPORTUNITIES for TEACHERS to COLLABORATE and LEARN FROM ONE ANOTHER

EXPERIMENT

PEER LEARNING

PLANNING

SHARED VISION AND INSTRUCTIONAL LANGUAGE

BALANCING AUTONOMY and SHARED VISION

INSTITUTIONAL LEARNING

SHARING INNOVATIVE PRACTICES with TEACHERS in LEADERSHIP ROLES

Some kids liked to be right on the merry-go-round getting spun around dizzy, and other kids liked to be on the ground, spinning the merry-go-round right round. A really good spinner had a few different moves. To get the merry-go-round started, you put your arms and shoulders against one of the metal rods and ran around with it. Eventually the flywheel spun so fast that you couldn't run around with it, and so you stood an arm's length away, slapping the metal rods to keep the momentum going. With the right timing and force, you could get the merry-go-round spinning very fast. If there were new kids—young kids—who hadn't played with the merry-go-round yet, a good spinner might show them how it worked by spinning the merry-go-round, then jumping on and sitting there a bit, then jumping off as it slowed to start pushing again.

In schools, the instructional leadership team—the principals, department heads, coaches, and other folks who serve teachers—are the spinners of the Cycle of Experiment and Peer Learning. The real game of the merry-go-round is on the spinning metal platform: huddling close to the bar when you are new and leaning out like a maniac with your hair flying out away from your head when you are more experienced. But for some kids, there comes a point in your playground career where you get a different kind of satisfaction from being the spinner and helping the folks on the merry-go-round enjoy that ride.

In this chapter, I describe four ways that instructional leaders can be the spinners for teachers and students in the Cycle of Experiment and Peer Learning. For those who are not in classrooms, your goal is to get the Cycle of Experiment and Peer Learning spinning as freely, joyfully, and collaboratively as possible. There are four places where the spinner can stand, push, run, and cheer to get the Cycle spinning more freely.

First, how can you create resources for **research and development** that will accelerate new experiments? How can you create more time for teachers? How can you give them more access to expertise and coaching to be able to adopt and invent new kinds of experiments?

Second, how can you create the conditions for **team learning**? How do you get teachers inside one another's classrooms to review what these small teams of folks conducting experiments are doing and to learn from those experiences?

Third, once you get some innovations that seem to be taking hold, how do you make sure there are opportunities for **institutional learning**? If teachers primarily adopt new practices based on what they learn from other teachers, how can you create conditions for that peer-to-peer learning?

Then the final piece that school leaders can do to help supervise this whole cycle is to think about how you create the conditions for a **shared vision and a shared instructional language**. How can you find language that helps teachers talk across grades and disciplines about what good teaching and learning looks like? In a school full of interesting classroom experiments, how do you create coherence across individual efforts, so the whole is greater than the sum of its parts?

Answering these questions is our work together in this chapter.

CREATING MORE OPPORTUNITIES FOR EXPERIMENTATION

Since classroom teachers (and other educators who work directly with students, like therapists, counselors, librarians, paraprofessionals, and so on) are the only people who can really lead instructional innovation, it matters greatly how much time, energy, and support that student-facing educators have for experimenta- tion. Much of the work of school leaders and other folks who aren't in the classroom is figur- ing out how to help teachers get time and resources for impor- tant work. Another crucial role is ensuring that teachers feel like they work in a culture in which

they are invited to step up into leadership roles. Dan Callahan is a longtime advocate for teacher-led professional development as one of the founders of EdCamps (more on that later) and as a professional development lead for the Massachusetts Teachers Association. He reminds us that management is a specifically administrative function, but leadership can be anywhere:

> *Leadership is different from management. A strong school admin-*
> *istrator, principal, or superintendent has daily management*
> *functions that they need to accomplish. But the real opportunity*
> *for leadership is thinking of ways that they can make sure that*
> *everybody in the building can assume leadership.*

Here are a few strategies for creating environments in which teachers have support for innovation and opportunities to lead.

POINTING A LIGHT: TARGETS OF DIFFICULTY

In my work helping educators use technology, teachers were often interested in experimenting with online tools for learning, but they didn't know where to start. My Harvard colleague Stone Wiske, author of the Teaching for Understanding framework, introduced me to the idea of a *target of difficulty*. A target of difficulty is a good place to think about trying something new, and it sits at the intersection of three features. The first is that what you're trying to teach and have students learn should be important. Invest innovation time in the things most worth learning. The second idea is that the place to try something new should be difficult to teach. If you've got some unit or lesson or part of your curriculum that's working extremely well, that's not the place to start. The place to start is in the parts of your curriculum that you're not satisfied with or you're not seeing the learning outcomes or growth that you were expecting. The third feature is that the domain should be some place where new technology or innovation might offer leverage for finding new solutions. A target of difficulty sits at the intersection of learning that's important, learning that's hard, and a place where innovation and experimentation might lead to better ideas. I've found with this framework that many teachers can think of a lesson, a unit, or a routine that would make for a good target of difficulty.[1]

MAKING TIME: SUMMER INNOVATION FUNDING

One of the most important things that school leaders can do is to help teachers find time for creative work. Leaders can be creative with professional development days, staffing times like lunch and recess, and using various meeting times throughout the school year. But teachers also have a big chunk of time during the summer where they can be hired to do innovation work.

The Leadership Public Schools in California had an interesting dilemma that illustrates a creative use of funding for teacher time in the summer. They primarily serve Spanish-speaking families whose children are learning English. The California higher education system requires students to have a minimum set of coursework in subjects like math and science to be able to enroll in college. When the Leadership Public Schools put English language learners (ELLs) in these courses, the students often struggled with academic English. But if they were pulled out of those courses for additional English instruction, the students wouldn't graduate with enough credits for college admission.

School leaders decided that they needed curriculum materials where academic English support was threaded through and embedded in these core math and science classes. They couldn't find publishers that had designed those materials, so they decided to develop their own. They paid teachers to develop materials over the summer using CK-12's free, open source, customizable Flex Books. Starting with an Algebra I course, they built lessons on academic English for mathematics directly into the course, so students could build their language skills while staying on track for a college-eligible diploma. They had good success with the course and continued in the years afterwards to swap out an expensive publisher curriculum for a teacher-developed curriculum that was designed to meet their needs.[2]

More simply, the Leadership Public Schools swapped out some of the textbook budget for teacher time, and with hard work and collaboration, they got learning materials that worked better for their students.

FINDING THE RESOURCES ALL AROUND YOU: STUDENTS AS DESIGNERS

Burlington, Massachusetts had one of the first high schools in the country to start a one-to-one program where every student had a computing device. High school principal Patrick Larkin quickly realized that even if they could afford the devices, they would never be able to bring their IT staffing up to levels to support those devices. Industry experts recommend a 70:1 ratio of employees to IT help desk staff. Count all of the students, faculty, and administrators in your school, and then count the number of IT staff devoted to direct support of those folks, and my hunch is that you'll find your ratio much, much less favorable.

Pat Larkin recognized that his school was full of people who loved tinkering with computers: students. So along with the 1:1 initiative, he and his colleagues set up a student help desk. In the early days, it was mostly focused on simple tech support. You could send a text or a tweet, and a sophomore would come dashing into your room to change your projector bulb or help you with a login problem. But over time, Burlington staff realized that students could be great partners in innovation. They set up a "genius bar" where teachers could reserve time with students who were deeply interested in education technology tools. Teachers would bring curriculum goals and ideas to the meeting, and students would help educators figure out how technology could help them meet their goals.[3]

The Quest to Learn School is a public middle school in New York City that developed a game-based curriculum for all its courses—final exams and projects are called "Boss Battles." They had a curriculum design team that was based out of an office in the middle of the school, and the doors were always open. Students would wander in and ask the design staff about new and upcoming units, and the staff would ask students to give their feedback and reviews on ideas in progress. I love that image of ongoing learning design where students are wandering in and out of the process.[4]

Your school is chock-full of students who would love to help your faculty make teaching and learning more engaging and productive. How can you create opportunities for them to help?

INNOVATION STAFFING: DEPARTMENT HEADS, COACHES, AND TEACHERS ON SPECIAL ASSIGNMENT

Another way to create opportunities for experimentation is to have more teachers on staff with part-time classroom teaching responsibilities and part of their time devoted to innovation work. Once you recognize that instructional innovations are developed by classroom teachers and shared by classroom teachers, then having people with part-time teaching responsibilities starts to make a lot of sense. There are good reasons to have full-time instructional coaches and full-time school staff devoted to teacher support, but it's important to realize two things about these kinds of full-time staff. First, they tend to be hired into roles focused on innovation and teacher support, but they can often get pulled into the daily work of filling staffing gaps and putting out fires. In 2021–2022, my lab at MIT worked with a group of instructional coaches across the Boston Public Schools, and when the Omicron wave of the coronavirus hit mid-year, all of them got pulled into substitute teaching rather than coaching. Second, once full-time instructional support staff spend a few years in those roles, they stop being viewed as practicing classroom teachers, so they lose some of their charisma and credibility in sharing ideas with other teachers.

Another strategy for ramping up innovation is buying out part of a teacher's time. Some schools have had these kinds of roles for many years; for instance, it's common for department heads to teach only two or three sections instead of five or six. Often, that time can get wrapped up in administrative responsibilities, so the challenge of school leaders is to minimize that bureaucracy and help department heads, part-time instructional coaches, or other part-time teachers devote their extra time to innovation and sharing ideas with peers. There is a job title that I first heard in California that I quite like: "teacher on special assignment," shortened to TOSA. A teacher on special assignment steps away from full-time teaching for a year or a few years to tackle some innovation project before returning to some classroom role. These roles can be a great way to reward teachers who are leaders in instructional innovation.

USING THE BULLY PULPIT

Finally, a crucial feature of experimentation is that it doesn't always work. Sometimes it takes a few tries to calibrate an idea and get it right. Some new ideas that seem terrific prove to be deeply flawed in practice. It's normal for experiments to go awry, and it's normal for those failed efforts to lead to frustration for students, parents, and teachers themselves.

But as educators, we don't want students to stick with the safe road in their learning. We don't want them to get stuck in only using learning and schooling strategies that have worked for them in the past and being skeptical and hesitant about new learning approaches. And if we want students to see the value of trying new approaches and testing new ideas, then they need to see educators making the same efforts.

School leaders can use their bully pulpit to encourage a culture of innovation. For many years, I facilitated year-long consultancies with schools where we pulled together a team of 10 to 20 teachers to work in a community of practice around technology innovation.[5] Whenever possible, we always pulled in the superintendent or principal to come to the first meeting to offer a benediction of sorts and lend their encouragement to the effort. It was also important for school leaders to reassure educators that they would defend teachers when things inevitably went sideways. Here's Kate Lewis's former superintendent, Mary Beth Banios, describing that support:

> *One of the really critical things about administration sup-*
> *porting teachers who want to be innovators is that they are*
> *encouraging the risk taking and being sure that they're cover-*
> *ing [teachers] when they fail. That whenever you do something*
> *innovative or you're trying to solve a problem, there is no chance*
> *that you're not going to do something that doesn't go well. And*
> *when that moment happens, it's critical that the administrator*
> *has the teacher's back. And they are explaining the type of work*
> *the teacher is engaged in and the value that work has to its stu-*
> *dents even when it fails.*

I want to be clear that many teachers will naturally be skeptical of the idea that administrators will cover for them when they fail, and that failure will be okay. I once visited a school in New Hampshire that was working toward schoolwide approaches to competency-based learning. English, science, and history had made great progress, but the math department was moving more slowly. I watched a conversation where the principal was speaking with two math teachers helping lead the effort, promising them that if things didn't work so well when it started, he'd have their back and it would be okay. It was obvious from the anxiety in their eyes that these teachers didn't quite believe him, or at least they knew that no matter what he said, if things got off to a rocky start, it would feel lousy for a while.

None of the strategies that I suggest here are magic solutions. One of the things I discuss in the next section on Design Thinking for Leading and Learning is how we can find small entry points for experimentation. When we organize change around quick and itera-tive cycles, that lowers the cost of experimentation and the conse-quences of failures and false starts.

MAKING TEAM LEARNING RICHER: LOOKING AT STUDENT WORK AND INSTRUCTIONAL ROUNDS

As instructional experiments are proceeding and wrapping up, we want to make sure that the people nearest to those experiments can learn from them in the Experience phase of the Cycle of Experiment and Peer Learning. Two of the most promising strategies for improving instructional team learning are looking at student work and instructional rounds, a particular form of classroom visits.

THE PROOF IN THE PUDDING: LOOKING AT STUDENT WORK

If a teaching innovation is working, you might see it in classroom discussion or individual interactions with students, but one of the most important places to look for the impact of change is in student work. If you are finding new ways to teach online research, do you see richer and more varied sources cited in student work? If you are teaching students about precision in measurements in science class, do you see more precise data recorded in lab reports? If new teaching practices are working, we should see the fruits of those efforts in student work.

Looking at student work involves closely examining representative pieces of student work and asking questions about what kinds of learning students are doing and what kinds of evidence we can find of student learning in their assessments. Teams usually use specific protocols that help keep people focused on evidence of student thinking and understanding. I'm partial to a set of tools from the National School Reform Faculty called the ATLAS protocol. It involves gathering a small group of educators to help a teacher reflect on what they can learn from a piece of student work that might come out of an instructional experiment.[6]

After a group of faculty members reads a sample of student work from an assignment, they meet for about an hour and follow a six-step protocol. First, the classroom teacher describes the assignment without making any claims about the student or the work. At this point, the focal teacher remains quiet for the next few steps. Second, the group starts a discussion by making what are called "low-inference observations." We'll discuss these more when we talk about the Collaborative Innovation Cycle, but these involve observing details in student work or in a classroom without passing judgment about them. It just asks people to look closely at details that seem important before leaping to assumptions about what a student might be thinking.

Once some of these details have been brought out, the group shifts to having a discussion around the question "From the student's perspective, what is the student working on?" It's most helpful to assume that the student is working in good faith and that, no matter how confusing things may look to educators, the work makes sense to the student. The goal is to understand what that sense is before passing any kind of judgment about the student or the assignment.

The next step, having understood what the student is working on, is to consider the question "What are the implications for teaching and assessment?" What kinds of teaching changes or new teaching approaches might help this student? What do you feel was missing from this student's assignment or what would you like to see in future work? After discussing these more interpretive questions, the focal teacher rejoins the discussion. They can share what they heard and learned from the conversation, and they can also provide the group with more background on the classroom activities and the student learning journey.

As teams get more proficient with the protocol, they can look at larger samples of student work or proceed through the process more quickly. Many educators come to really enjoy the process of looking at student work to try to understand student thinking before leaping ahead to thinking about iterating on new approaches to teaching.

GETTING INTO CLASSROOMS: INSTRUCTIONAL ROUNDS

In a workshop, I once had an assistant principal explain that they made the following offer to their faculty: "Any time you want to visit someone else's classroom, let me know and I'll come cover your class." The AP went on to explain that typical classroom routines often include class periods like independent project work and quizzes where he could easily sit in class, get his work done, and students could proceed with minimal support. During these periods, the AP encouraged teachers to call on him to sit with the class, so that teachers could visit each other.

I have a very distinct memory of a teacher on the other side of the room, jaw dropped, saying something like, "You do that for your teachers?" The offer was so simple, and especially in a world of networked laptops, it seemed so easy for the AP to continue his work, visit with some students, get a pulse check on the school, and help his teachers get around the building.

Any chance to get teachers into each other's classrooms is good, but we can do even better. Like looking at student work, instructional rounds are a structured protocol for doing classroom observations. As with looking at student work, there are published protocols for these activities that can help; the book *Instructional Rounds* by Elizabeth City and colleagues is a useful guide. Ideally, you'd have a small group of teachers working together on some innovation initiative. Then, a few of them and a few other teachers would go on rounds together, visiting classrooms for about 20–25 minutes each classroom, with a problem of practice to focus on that relates to the innovation. If the experiments focused on formative assessment, the problem of practice might be something like, "How are teachers tracking student learning and using that information in class?"[7]

Again, observers start by taking low-inference notes, trying to document what they see in the classrooms without making too many assumptions or judgments. After observing several classrooms, teachers gather and discuss. They start at the low-inference level, talking about details of their observations, then proceed to an analysis phase looking at patterns, trends, and interesting anomalies. The final step in the process is to make predictions: "If you were a student in these classes and did everything the teacher asked you to do, what would you have learned?" As with looking at student work, the goal is to try to understand the experience from students' perspectives before shifting toward thinking about strategies for improvement.

In many schools, classroom observation has become so closely linked to evaluation processes that a taboo develops about visiting classrooms. But it's incredibly difficult to learn about teaching without seeing other people do it! Recently, I saw a group of teachers on Twitter post pictures of signs on their door that said something along the lines of "Visitors Welcome! I'm looking for feedback on X, Y, Z," which was a wonderfully inviting way to create a stronger culture of teacher sharing.

The team learning that constitutes the Experience phase of the Cycle of Experiment and Peer Learning will happen whether school leaders intentionally support the process or not. Teachers talk! And they enjoy talking about what they are doing, what they are trying, and what's working. But making time for instructional rounds or looking at student work can help that reflection happen more frequently. And introducing teachers to these kinds of formal protocols can help that reflection happen more intentionally.

INSTITUTIONAL LEARNING: RAMPING UP PLANNING THROUGH PEER-TO-PEER LEARNING

After teachers conduct experiments and reflect with small groups of colleagues on what they've learned, the next step is giving teachers time to share their newfound expertise across schools, districts, and broader groups of educators. Remember, teachers report that the number-one influence on their pedagogy is other teachers. If we want teaching and learning to improve, that will only happen when educators get exposed to new ideas and insights that come from their colleagues.

Again, Dan Callahan has a worthwhile perspective on peer learning:

Teacher-to-teacher learning is important because your peers are the experts who are on the ground with you learning things through their own hard-won experience. And giving teachers the opportunity and the ability and the freedom to share their expertise is incredibly valuable. It's valuable both for giving teachers who don't have some of those experiences the opportunity to learn from those who do, but also to elevate our understanding of what that experience means to the person who's in the classroom and has won it through their own work. I think we don't frequently enough celebrate the hard work that goes into becoming an excellent teacher. And one of the most powerful ways that we can really do that is by giving our expert educators the opportunity to share their learning with other peers.

Administrators are in a really unique place to help facilitate teacher-to-teacher learning, in that they can do two things in my opinion. They can really set the tone for the community. Because with teachers, just like with their students, there needs to be an aspect of trust and a real relationship there in order for people to be able to be willing to learn from each other. Principals also have the ability to work on schedules and make sure that there are real opportunities for teachers to be able to share with each other. And so that could be using professional development and staff meeting time in a less formal way, so that teachers are encouraged to share with each other. Or it could mean really taking a look at the way that the school day is structured and arranging it in such a way that teachers have more opportunities to interact with each other.

The following are a few specific ways of making good on Dan's important suggestions.

MEETING TIMES ARE INSTRUCTIONAL SHARING TIMES

Look at your annual calendar of meetings: faculty meetings, grade-level meetings, department meetings, professional learning communities (PLCs), professional development days, and so on. How many minutes of those meetings are devoted to bureaucratic issues, and how much of that time could be converted into discussion and sharing about teaching? How much of the bureaucratic work in meetings could be addressed through handouts or other written communication, in order to make more time sharing about pedagogy?

There are lots of tricks for making more time for teachers to talk about teaching. Perhaps the most effective is setting boundaries around meetings, ensuring that some time is *always* devoted to teaching and learning. During the first two years of the pandemic, schools faced unprecedented, rapid changes, both in the organization of school and in our approaches to instruction. Nichole Allard in the Vista Public Schools recognized that in every faculty meeting, the organizational issues were taking up the entire meeting, so they switched to a schedule of alternating between organizational and instructional topics for meeting agendas. The instructional time required defending—there are always fires that need to be put out—but two things turned out to be true. First, instructional improvements are a means of addressing other kinds of school challenges: when teaching is richer, more relevant, and more compelling, it can solve underlying problems with attendance, engagement, community conflict, and so forth. Second, meetings will take up as much time as we give them, and often it's a good experiment to see if bureaucratic time can be reduced without really compromising organizational effectiveness.

Department meetings and grade-level meetings are great targets for shifting conversations to instruction. In my first teaching job, our history department decided to shift more of our meeting time to discussing teaching. We started by calling these sessions "Best Practices" but quickly decided to shift the name to "Practices" because we realized we often wanted to talk about what we were doing that wasn't working or maybe could be working one day but wasn't there yet.

Sometimes with some modest incentives, you can help teachers find a little more time to engage with each other. In the very first urban school in the United States to have a one-to-one laptop program, the Lila G. Frederick Pilot School in Boston, the principal, Deb Socia, started a weekly event called "Bagels and Laptops." She bought a big spread of bagels, cream cheese, and coffee, and invited teachers to come in a little early for breakfast one day a week. The agenda was to have one teacher share something new that they were doing with technology that week. (When tablets spread through schools, some places named these kinds of instructional sharing meetings Appy Hours.) The program was low cost and a light lift for everyone involved, but it helped create a stronger culture of curiosity, sharing, and peer-to-peer learning.

TEACHER-LED PEER-TO-PEER LEARNING

As educators know all too well, an extraordinary amount of teacher professional learning is organized around outside consultants or administrators lecturing to teachers. It's not fun, and the evidence on its efficacy is quite mixed.[8] If teachers primarily learn from other teachers, then one question we can ask is, "How might we make our professional learning more teacher-led?"

One of my favorite teacher learning events was at the back-to-school professional development event of the Peel School Board in Ontario. I gave a talk in the morning, and there were teacher-led breakout sessions throughout the day. The school is organized around a giant hallway (like many cold-weather school buildings), with a big atrium in the middle. The organizers set up a buffet lunch in the atrium and then lined the hallway with  tables. During lunch the tables were set up like a science fair, but instead it was a teaching fair. Educators showed off lesson plans, student work from projects, and digital learning activities, and the rest of the school faculty wandered up and down the halls chatting, looking at projects, and starting small conversations. A giant celebration of innovative teaching is my kind of way to start the year!

Another way to ensure that faculty lead professional development is to put them in charge of organizing it. For over a decade, the Watertown School District in Massachusetts has made teacher leadership a pillar of their year-round professional learning design. A faculty-led group of educators organizes the programming for the year. Programs are typically blended, with some online components, some meetings throughout the year, and then some deeper dives on professional development days. Nearly all the programming is led by teachers, so to meet your requirement you either agree to lead a strand, or you join one. There were also options for individual or small group study, for educators who wanted to work together on something specific.

One way to both kickstart and sustain teacher-led professional development is through EdCamps.[9] The EdCamp model was developed by a group of Philadelphia educators (including Dan Callahan) who visited an "unconference" put together by technology developers. In an unconference, people gather in a place with plenty of meeting rooms and no set agenda. The day starts by having people propose topics for discussion and sharing. Typically, there is a big whiteboard with a grid with meeting rooms as columns and times as rows, and the grid slowly gets populated with topics. Someone takes a picture, sends it around electronically to everyone, and then people start gathering. Sometimes folks take on roles volunteering as facilitators, but the idea is never to have people lecturing on topics but rather to give as many people in the room as possible time and space to share. The EdCamp folks realized this unconference model could be very powerful with educators, and they did some pilots, and ultimately started an organization to help others organize EdCamps. The model took off, and now just about every day of the year, some-one somewhere is hosting an EdCamp: https://digitalpromise.org/edcamp/attend/.

OUTSIDE EXPERTISE AS THE CATALYST TO PEER-TO-PEER LEARNING

I started this chapter with a warning about outside consultants, and their limits in driving change. But I do think outside consultants can be helpful to schools. In fact, I ran a consultancy for about 15 years! But our primary model for our professional learning services was to assume that our credibility with most teachers was limited.

Our main offering to schools was a year-long blended pro-fessional learning program where we primarily worked with a small group of 10–20 teacher-leaders. It wasn't important whether these folks had any particular expertise or existing leadership posi-tions—we imagined leadership emerging from everywhere—but it was important that our participants were really eager to learn about technology integration or whatever topic we were hired to help with. As outsiders, we worked with those teacher leaders both to improve the teaching in their own classrooms and to strengthen their skills in sharing what they learned with others. As we did these year-long programs, we sometimes also did whole-school keynotes and workshops and typical kinds of professional development. But we had a healthy respect for the limits of what we could do from outside the community, and we focused on building strong internal capacity for iterative improvement and change.[10]

Again, if teachers conduct most instructional experiments that lead to improvement, and if teachers primarily learn from other teachers, then instructional improvement occurs when teachers have the time and freedom to experiment and the time and support to share what they've learned with others.

ROWING IN THE SAME DIRECTION: CREATING COMMON INSTRUCTIONAL LANGUAGE AND A SHARED VISION

Good design often involves balancing tensions. Throughout this chapter, I've emphasized the vital importance of teacher leadership. But there are lots of teachers in schools, and if they focus all their learning, growth, and improvement on idiosyncratic goals, then it's hard for groups of teachers to improve. In lots of places, teachers make substantial improvements

in teaching in their own individual classrooms, but those improvements don't lead to better grade levels, better departments, or better schools. A measure of individual teacher leadership, autonomy, and agency is good and vital for motivation—after all, teachers are probably taking on these leadership and improvement opportunities without much in the way of financial or career rewards. However, that autonomy and agency is best balanced with a sense of shared purpose. Faculty learning works best when it is like an orchestra, where individual musicians are constantly refining their technique but also working collaboratively toward a shared performance.[11]

While unleashing individual leadership is one role for school leadership, another role is trying to harness that energy in a common direction. There are two kinds of tools for creating that common direction: a shared instructional language and a shared vision.

PREPARING TO COMMUNICATE TOGETHER: CREATING A COMMON INSTRUCTIONAL LANGUAGE

Teaching is immensely complex and nuanced, and the work of teaching is incredibly diverse. A fifth-grade science teacher might have deep content knowledge in earth science and life science, and a kindergarten teacher might have a better understanding of developing number sense and the foundations of literacy. The way those two teachers understand the work of teaching, the ways they were trained to teach, their experiences with young people, and the ways they talk about teaching all can be very different.

One way to help faculty speak together and collaborate across these kinds of differences is to adopt a shared instructional language. By instructional language, I mean a framework for talking and thinking about teaching and learning. Understanding by Design, by Jay McTighe and Grant Wiggins, is an instructional language organized around curriculum planning and backwards design. Teaching for Understanding, by faculty and researchers at Harvard's Project Zero, offers a similar framework with an emphasis on connecting individual lessons to big year-long themes. Universal Design for Learning is an instructional language that emphasizes designing learning environments to support the diverse needs of learners. Teach Like a Champion is an instructional framework for maximizing classroom time and efficiency that is widely used in some charter school networks. The International Baccalaureate program is a curriculum system that also includes an instructional language. Many school systems create their own instructional languages. The Long Beach Unified School District in California has an Understandings Curriculum to guide instructional planning and evaluation (https://www.lbschools.net/departments/curriculum/curriculum-services/excellence-and-equity/understanding-curriculum). High Tech High, a charter school network in San Diego, has a PBL Design Kit for introducing new teachers and visitors to their approach to project-based learning.[12]

I have some thoughts and opinions about these various approaches, but my strongest position is this: your school should adopt one of these. **It's not so important to pick the one right system as it is to get one system right**. Pick one book or set of resources that everyone in your school reads together, so that you have some common language for talking about learning design, teaching, and assessment.

My colleagues Jal Mehta (from Harvard) and Sara Fine (from the High Tech High Graduate School of Education) wrote a book called *In Search of Deeper Learning* where they visited a project-based high school, an International Baccalaureate school, and a no-excuses charter school. What they found was that all these schools were quite different in their approaches to teaching and learning, but they also all had the capacity to create powerful learning experiences for students. What these great schools shared was their commitment to continuously improving teaching and having a shared framework for educators to talk about and collaborate around.[13]

For schools that are just starting to come together around an instructional language, it certainly makes sense to collaborate with teachers and school leaders to figure out what approach people are most excited about and might help them best improve. But the crucial decision is not which framework to pick, but rather how a shared instructional language can help educators talk together and collaborate.

DEVELOPING A SHARED VISION: RIGHT-SIZED GOALS

Ideally, as teachers are conducting experiments in their individual classrooms, all those discrete experiences add up to a richer, more coherent learning experience for students. For idiosyncratic experiments to add up to something bigger, schools need to have some sense of common focus. I've come to call well-designed areas of focus as "right-sized goals," which are goals that might take anywhere from one to four years to work on and are specific enough that they are tractable but broad enough that people in different departments and teaching specialties can see themselves inside the work.

In the early 2000s, a common goal for schools was to work on twenty-first-century skills, which always struck me as too broad to be "right-sized." School leaders would say that they wanted all teachers to incorporate the 4Cs of creativity, collaboration, critical thinking, and communication into every lesson. While each of those components is a laudable goal, thinking that every teacher would get good at all those things in a short period of time is just unrealistic. That might make for a good long-term mission, but it's not focused enough to serve as a guide for coordinated improvement.

In the Common Core era, my hometown of Arlington, Massachusetts came up with what I thought were some nice district-wide goals for instructional improvement. The assistant superintendent told me that in the early grades they wanted to focus on getting students ready to learn: improving executive function, self-talk and self-regulation, and collaboration. They adopted a curriculum called Tools of the Mind across their elementary schools to help teachers address these challenges. In the secondary grades, they thought that some of the best parts of the then-new Common Core standards related to reasoning from evidence and thinking through how evidence builds toward arguments.

These are goals that are broad enough that nearly every teacher can see themselves within them. A kindergarten teacher can be implementing the Tools of the Mind curriculum, and fifth-grade teachers can think about how they build on those foundational skills toward greater independence. Across the subjects and disciplines, reasoning from evidence is specific enough that it involves a tractable number of ideas and possible teaching approaches but broad enough that most teachers across math, science, English, history, and the other essentials can see themselves in the conversation.

Because I live in town, I had more opportunities to test whether this was pie-in-the-sky district office talk or really the lived work of teachers. I met a seventh-grade science teacher out walking his dog in my neighborhood and asked him about the reasoning and discourse work, and he assured me that it was really going on. "Actually, the Science and English teachers just got together and realized that we were using words like 'hypothesis,' 'warrant,' and 'evidence' very differently in our subjects, and our kids are confused! So, we're figuring out what to do about that." When a random teacher in my neighborhood can talk that specifically about cross-department collaboration on an initiative prescribed by the superintendent, that's good evidence that people are moving in the same direction.

Ideally, faculty work on these right-sized goals for a couple of years, and then innovation just becomes routine practice. My own kids entered the elementary school several years after these areas of focus, and when my daughters started kindergarten and first grade, they just did the Tools of the Mind curriculum, and their teachers introduced it not as a special innovation, but as a well-established way to help kids get adjusted to their life and work in schools. At that point, the elementary schools had picked another right-sized goal, getting students to adopt more diverse problem-solving approaches in math classes, and they were once again adopting new curriculum and shifting their practices one grade level at a time. When districts can create right-sized goals, meet them, and move on to new ones, that's powerful evidence of teachers and school leaders collaborating and iteratively improving.

ITERATING FORWARD WITH THE CYCLE OF EXPERIMENT AND PEER LEARNING

In Chapter 1, I made a point that the Cycle of Experiment and Peer Learning came out of observations and interviews and an approach to research called *descriptive research*. When I first started these observations, I wasn't necessarily trying to make schools better; I was just trying to understand a puzzle that I observed. Lots of schools bought technology at that time, and in most places, it didn't seem to make much difference in instruction outside of a few special classrooms, but in some places it seemed like technology was a catalyst for real building-wide or district-wide change.

The Cycle of Experiment and Peer Learning helped me understand why some places got so much more instructional improvement from these technology investments. Teaching and learning improves where teachers feel free and supported to experiment and they have opportunities to share their learning with others. As that sharing takes place, there are more educators who are more willing to try versions of those same experiments, and new practices build, spread, and improve throughout the faculty.

As this chapter tries to show, educators who are outside the classroom have many actions that they can take to make this cycle spin more productively, more efficiently, more collaboratively, and more joyfully. But the starting point for this work is recognizing that a top-down mandate for something like greater use of technology isn't top-down in practice. Ultimately, the adoption of new tools or new approaches and their true integration into teaching practice only happens through teacher leadership and teacher peer-to-peer learning.

The next two sections present two more cycles: Design Thinking for Leading and Learning and the Collaborative Innovation Cycle. My colleagues and I designed these two models intending for them to be prescriptive rather than descriptive. They are more about how schools could be, although both models try to respect where schools are, and especially to respect the vital role of teacher leadership in instructional change.

Design Thinking for Leading and Learning attempts to provide more clarity about how educators might approach instructional experiments most effectively. In this chapter on the Cycle of Experiment and Peer Learning, I've discussed how important these experiments are, but my observational research didn't really offer many clues about the best way to do them. Design Thinking for Leading and Learning offers a framework to help teachers think about experiments, with a particular focus on trying to make initial experiments simple, quick, and inexpensive to run, so that failures come with low costs of time, energy, and disruption. When we make failure cheap, we can iterate more courageously to new things that work.

Whereas Design Thinking for Leading and Learning zooms in on classroom experiments, the Collaborative Innovation Cycle pans out to particular focus on the last of our topics here: How do we create a shared vision for change? What kinds of thinking, reading, conversations, and exercises can help a community find their way toward a right-sized goal? The Collaborative Innovation Cycle offers a framework for thinking about how to get communities working on innovation together.

DESIGN THINKING
FOR LEADING AND LEARNING

CHAPTER

3

WHAT IS DESIGN THINKING?

Design thinking is a systemic approach to solving complex problems through iterative cycles of inquiry, prototyping, and testing. This kind of tinkering is fundamental to the human experience. The first stone tools were assuredly developed by sorting through rock shards, imaging new possibilities for those shards, trying out different rocks and ways of shaping stones, and refining techniques for cutting and digging. Tinkering is timeless; however, in recent decades designers, engineers, philosophers, and educators have thought more systematically about design and have developed steps and protocols that make design thinking more accessible and useful.

If you have found your way to this book, it's likely that you have run into ideas about design thinking. I knew design thinking was surging in education circles when *The Atlantic* published an article in 2017, "How Design Thinking Became a Buzzword at School." The premise of the article was that design thinking was growing in popularity in schools but was new and untested and might prove to be another passing fad.[1] Parts of that diagnosis struck me as fair: design thinking was new to schools and plenty of applications and some efforts would be disappointing.

But sitting on my perch at MIT, design thinking didn't look like a passing fad; it looked like the toolkit that researchers in my lab used every day to try to improve teaching and learning. It looked like the methods that my colleagues used every day across the university—from computational biology to mechanical engineering to digital humanities—to try to build better futures. Rather than a passing fad, iterative approaches to exploring, prototyping, testing, and refining seemed fundamental to the future of all kinds of science and engineering.

Design thinking has two promising applications in schools. First, it's a useful set of skills for students to learn. If your students graduate to places like MIT, they are likely to end up in a major or program where they use design thinking every day. Second, it's a powerful set of ideas for addressing the problems that come up in classroom teaching and in running schools and districts. Design thinking is useful to teach our students for their future work, and it's useful to use with students and colleagues to make schools better.

Design thinking isn't one single thing; it's a set of mindsets, techniques, and protocols. My colleagues and I at the Teaching Systems Lab—especially Blake Sims, Elizabeth Huttner, and Alyssa Napier—developed our own flavor of the design process, which we called Design Thinking for Leading and Learning. The two Ls at the end,

Leading and Learning, were meant to emphasize that design thinking is useful for teaching in and changing schools. We co-taught an online course called Design Thinking for Leading and Learning, which you can find at MIT's Open Learning Library. (Go to openlearninglibrary. mit.edu and search for "Design Thinking for Leading and Learning" or go direct to https://openlearninglibrary.mit.edu/courses/course-v1:MITx+11.155x+1T2019/about.) The next two chapters borrow greatly from that online course, and nearly all of the materials in the online course are available for sharing and reuse under a Creative Commons CC:BY license.

Like every other approach to design thinking, we imagined design as an interactive cycle with a set of overlapping steps. We chose language for our six steps—Discover, Focus, Imagine, Proto-type, Try, and Reflect and Share—that we thought would be sensi-ble for adults but also understandable to children. We tried to avoid terms that might be confusing in education. For instance, in many design-thinking models, people use the term "test" to refer to the step of evaluating prototypes, but the word "test" has a bit of a bad rap among students. Plenty of folks have "test anxiety," but there is much less "try anxiety."

In the previous chapters on the Cycle of Experiment and Peer Learning, I showed how experimentation is essential to instructional change, and I argued that schools that are good at improving are also good at fostering new teaching experiments. Design Thinking for Leading and Learning is a protocol and process, usable by both young students and their adult educators, for being strategic, deliber-ate, and skillful in conducting these kinds of experiments.

In this chapter, we start by looking at some of the recent history of design thinking, and we contrast iterative approaches to design with more linear approaches. I explain each of the six steps or phases in Design Thinking for Leading and Learning. Throughout this chapter, designers at MIT and people who work with schools explain how they go through the design process to address a wide range of problems.

One of the fun things about teaching design thinking in school is that nearly all educators have deep and useful intuitions about the process. Folks who teach science and math often feel comfortable with prototyping ideas, trying them out, examining results, and refining prototypes. Folks who teach English, history, and social studies are usually good at empathizing with people's challenges, identifying key problems in systems, and imagining new futures. Anyone who teaches writing has a good sense of drafting, offering feedback, and iterating. You are already a designer! Most of what we explore in this chapter offers another frame for applying skills that you have already developed in your teaching practice. In the next chapter, I share a set of activities and protocols that you can use with your students and colleagues to put design thinking to work with the problems that you care most about.

But let's start with a little history, because it turns out that the software revolution helps explain the recent surge in design thinking, and it also is fun to discover that one of the most widely respected philosophers in education was also essential to the origins of design thinking.

FROM WATERFALLS TO SPRINTS: A BRIEF HISTORY OF DESIGN

Sometimes when people want to solve big problems, they make a plan and then execute that plan. Since big problems are big, it makes sense to break those problems down into a series of steps. For many problems those steps might include: (1) establishing a goal, (2) defining specifications for success, (3) drawing a plan or blueprint, (4) collecting inputs and resources, (5) building the product, (6) stress testing the final product, and (7) wrapup and ongoing maintenance. When I think of the great infrastructure wonders of the twentieth century—the Hoover Dam or the Golden Gate Bridge—I imagine the planners using this kind of linear, step-by-step approach to design, planning, and execution.

On big projects, these steps are usually not perfectly sequential; the time allotted for each new step overlaps a bit with the previous step. One way to plot these steps visually is called a Gantt chart, developed by an industrial consultant in the early twentieth century for managing construction and production projects. The columns of a Gantt chart represent units of time, like a month, quarter, or year, and the rows correspond to steps of the project. These kinds of charts are also called Waterfall charts, because the shaded areas corresponding to the time allotted for each step juts out to the right of the previous step, looking like a set of cascades or a waterfall. Sometimes this whole linear, sequential approach to design is called a Waterfall process. If you look at most strategic planning documents that schools create, they tend to be inspired by this kind of design approach: Do X in Year 1, then Y in Year 2, and then Z in Year 3 to accomplish the goal.

Waterfall approaches to design have a signature vulnerability: if you make a mistake early in the process, that mistake gets baked into the rest of the design. What if your users, clients, or customers don't want your end goal? What if there are incorrect assumptions in your specifications for the final product? What if there are errors in the plan or blueprint? What if the world changes midway through your plan, and people no longer need what you are building? (Think of all the five-year strategic plans that schools published in 2019, right before the coronavirus pandemic.) Sometimes you can patch these kinds of errors along the way, but sometimes projects are saddled for their entire lifetimes with mistakes made at the beginning.

Relatively early in its evolution, the software industry recognized these problems with Waterfall approaches to design. Teams would take on large, multiyear, complex software projects, but the world would be changing around them. You spend five years building software to help bank tellers, but in that window most of your customers switch to using ATMs. You build a new online storefront for people to use with their computers, but in that window most of your customers switch to using their phones.[2]

One of the extraordinary, unheralded features of software is that deleting things is incredibly easy. A few keystrokes can remove hundreds of lines of code from a program, and a few more keystrokes can put them back in. You can't take out one of the pylons of the Golden Gate bridge for a redo or pull out a chunk of the Hoover Dam and see how things work without it for a few minutes. The software equivalent is surprisingly straightforward. (Importantly, lessons and curriculum share this quality: swapping lessons and units from year to year is more like changing code than replacing bridge foundations.)

Since early errors in a Waterfall approach are costly and deletions are easy, software engineers shifted toward more iterative approaches that have lots of names, but a good summary term is Agile design. Agile design replaces the long, linear structure of Waterfall with many short cycles, sometimes called sprints. A sprint is a working period, typically a few weeks in length, for new work to be launched, completed, and reviewed. In the early phases of a new project, sprints are usually working toward a "minimum viable product," the most basic version of a thing that allows designers to see whether an idea can work in the real world.

For instance, the ride-hailing app Uber started with a particularly vivid minimum viable product: the founders wanted users to be able to press a few buttons on their phone, walk out on the street, and have a black luxury sedan pick them up and drive them somewhere, feeling the whole time like a VIP. The minimum viable product was to have one small area in one city, serviced by a small number of car service companies, where this vision could come to life. (Uber then proved to be a permanently unprofitable menace to congestion, public transportation, municipal regulations, and society, but it still very nicely illustrates a minimum viable product.) Before they sold everything under the sun, Amazon's minimum viable product was shipping you a book from a large book catalog. The first Kickstarter project was funded for $35 by three backers, who paid a user called "darkpony" to draw pictures, including "a half dragon man with a pitchfork and some skulls and he is flying towards a city to wreck it. and maybe he has some smaller dragonpeople sidekicks flying alongside him" (sic).[3] From that one incredibly compelling experiment, a whole new field of artistic crowdfunding emerged.

In Agile design, the goal is to quickly build the most basic possible version of a new idea that lets you test its viability. Part of the goal here is to make failure cheap. One of the reasons we fear failure in education design is that our time for planning and experimenting is limited, so we want to use it well. We also don't want to impede young people's education with half-baked ideas that don't work as well as we hoped. One way to minimize these risks is to try to make our experiments quick, small, and light. If small things fail, it's okay, because we didn't put too much into them. If small things work, then that gives us the green light to build on and expand that idea.

In Agile development, after a minimum viable product seems to be working, ongoing development continues through sprints that add new features and capacity. Each feature is inspired by a design hypothesis, such as "If we build X, then users will have a better experience with Y." A good sprint explores the possibility space of a new idea, sets a design hypothesis, imagines solutions, prototypes those solutions, and then tests them. Instead of imagining development as one long waterfall, Agile builds large, complex projects through dozens of short, iterative sprints. As software has spread through-out every facet of government, economy, and social life, these ideas about iterative design have spread as well.

FILM, POLAROIDS, AND DIGITAL PHOTOS

Let me offer one more example of the shift to shorter, tighter spi-rals of creation and design: when I was a child at summer camp in the 1980s, one of the activity options was photography. We showed up in the darkroom and we were assigned a camera that we loaded with film. Now, for you younger readers, it used to be that when you wanted to take photographs with a camera, you had to insert a plastic roll that contained 24 or 36 squares of physical film.

We'd run all over camp, staging our friends in photographs or capturing moments of sailing, archery, and baseball with candid shots. We'd look down our lens, press a button to open the shutter, and let the light fall on our physical film for an instant to capture an image. And we would have *no idea* whether our pictures were any good.

A day or two later, when our turn for the photography activity came around again, we'd go to the darkroom and develop our rolls of film in big vats of chemicals. Hours later, as the prints dried, we'd finally get a chance to look at our photographs and see whether we had found the right vantage, understood the light, or captured the moment. And later in the summer we would head out with cameras again, having learned from past mistakes.

When Polaroid instant cameras were developed, photography took its first step toward a profound change. An instant camera was still loaded with physical film, but it would print an image right after you took the photograph. Now, you could compose a photograph, take a picture, and see what your print would look like in minutes. If you got the light or composition wrong, you didn't have to wait days to fix it; you could try again in the same place with the same subjects.

Nearly all of us now use digital cameras that make this cycle even faster. You take a picture, glance down at the screen, and see your photo. You can rearrange your subjects, find a new spot, or wait a few more minutes for the perfect light. The film that we developed—in traditional cameras or Polaroids—cost money, so we were often careful with the shots we took. But digital file space is now so inexpensive that we can take as many photos as we like, and we can instantly delete the ones that go awry.

As much as possible, we want our innovation efforts to feel more like digital photography than traditional photography. We want to design our experiments to try an innovation, take a quick snapshot of the process and results, and then make whatever big changes or small tweaks will guide us to even better results.

Among those who study product and service development, this kind of agile, iterative approach to imagining and building the future has a name: design thinking.

FROM DEWEY TO DESIGN THINKING

In a 1992 paper, Richard Buchanan, a professor of design at Carnegie Mellon University, wrote a paper called "Wicked Problems in Design Thinking" where he traced this history of design thinking, starting with a name very familiar to educators: John Dewey.[4] For Dewey, science in the twentieth century was marked by a transformational shift from the pure sciences—which tried to carefully observe nature to deduce its properties—to the applied sciences, where you figure things out in the world by building things and observing your creations. Dewey is renowned among educators both for his Lab School in Chicago where new ideas could be developed and tested and for believing that student learning should be defined by these same kinds of experiments and experiences. As Dewey famously said, "Education is not preparation for life, but life itself."[5] In some respects, the origins of design thinking in the United States are deeply connected to some of the most important and influential ideas in the history of education as well.

The term *design thinking* appeared in scholarly literature in the 1970s and 1980s, and it was later widely popularized by a consulting firm called Ideo, which integrated design thinking into product design. Ideo developed and codified a five-step model for design cycles: Empathize, Define, Ideate, Prototype, and Test. These ideas became central to the Stanford Design School, or d.school, which has become one of the driving forces of design education (teaching people to be designers) and in integrating design in education (teaching educators how to use design).

A key tenet of the Ideo/d.school approach to design is empathy. All too often, when designers encounter a problem, they leap to assumptions about how they as individuals would experience the problem or how they would solve it. A major part of the discipline of design thinking is restraining those early assumptions, tucking them away, and then spending a substantial amount of time trying to understand a problem from the perspectives of the people who encounter that problem every day. Lots of people become teachers because they liked school and were good at it. Lots of people choose their teaching subject because they find it intuitive, engaging, beautiful, or interesting. But many of our students are not big fans of our subjects or even of school at all. When we understand what teaching, learning, and school looks like from the perspectives of young people—from the perspectives of folks for whom school is not working so well—we're more likely to find our way to solutions that address those complex needs. Put another way, when we understand problems in the way that typical people do, we're more likely to be able to design solutions, approaches, and resources that address the problems that people have, not the problems that designers think they have.

Another description for this approach to design thinking is "human-centered design." Especially in product design—building furniture, computers, cleaning products, and other stuff—it's easy to think that what you are doing is making a thing better and to focus entirely on the design of that thing. But those products are used every day by people to engage in human activities and solve human problems. Human-centered design tries to shift product designers away from thinking about the products themselves, in isolation, and toward thinking more about how products are used by real humans in the world, hence "human-centered design." Chris Lehmann, the founder of Science Leadership Academy in Philadelphia, summarizes this distinction in a similar way for educators. "We don't teach physics, we teach kids physics."[6] From my own experience teaching history, I know that sometimes I designed a set of lecture slides thinking about how to accurately convey events and themes in some time period. That's all important, but I needed to do more than think about what I conveyed; I needed to imagine how students would understand my slides about some period. To do that, I couldn't just think like a historian, I needed to think like a student learning history; I couldn't just think about the slides as a product, I needed to think about how the slides were used by learners in my classroom context. Being accurate and being comprehensible are not the same!

THE DESIGN JUSTICE CRITIQUES OF DESIGN THINKING

As design thinking has been refined and grown in popularity, it's encountered all kinds of criticism. To me, the most important and valuable criticisms of design thinking have come from a group of people organized under the mantle of "design justice." Folks interested in design justice observe that too often designers pay insufficient attention to the long-term consequences of their design and the ways that power imbalances influence the design process.[7]

Some of the earliest advocates of design justice were in the disability rights movements, where activists argued, "Nothing about us without us." In many conversations about accommodations for buildings or transportation, new designs and regulations have been developed without leadership—sometimes without involvement—from people with disabilities. Folks with disabilities not only deserve to be included in design that involves them, but they have essential experience from their everyday lives about how accommodations work and don't. Many urban planners, civil engineers, architects, and other folks who design the spaces we live in, work from, and move through don't have disabilities, so it's incumbent upon them to involve people from the disabled community in their work as designers.[8]

Design justice starts from the stance that the best possible designs will include diverse perspectives throughout the design process: in exploring problems, imagining and testing solutions, and in reviewing and reflecting on outcomes from design. Design justice advocates typically don't reject human-centered design practices, but they do observe that the most powerful advocates of these practices are elite institutions; Ideo is a consulting firm that works with Fortune 500 companies and the d.school is at one of the world's most prestigious universities. Design Justice isn't necessarily about creating new steps in the design process, it's about ensuring that in each of those steps, designers consider who they are including in their work, how they evaluate the effects of their designs on different people, and how they observe and address the long-term consequences of their work. For example, homework policies and everyday homework decisions in your schools affect teachers, administrators, students, and students' families. When homework decisions negatively affect affluent parents, those parents have the work flexibility, time, and resources to advocate for their students and families and for different decisions. When homework decisions negatively affect working-class parents, they have different constraints on how they can advocate for change—it may be harder to get off a shift from work or they may have language barriers communicating with the school. Considering those differences and ensuring that different voices are included in design processes is an essential foundation to design justice.

GETTING STARTED WITH DESIGN THINKING FOR LEADING AND LEARNING

All of us are designers. Herbert Simon, one of the earliest advocates of the science of design at Carnegie Mellon, wrote that "everyone designs who devises courses of action."[9] We solve all kinds of problems every day. Some problems are personal and simple: To answer "How should I get to work today?," you make decisions about whether to take public transportation, if you have time to stop by the coffee shop, or how you can avoid traffic. Other problems are broader and more complex. How can I get students to learn and care about British literature or protecting the environment? Design thinking is a flexible and powerful approach to problem solving when we don't fully understand what the problem is, and we can't anticipate what solutions might look like in advance.

Designers often represent Design Thinking for Leading and Learning as a cycle, with other microcycles embedded within it. Another useful way to think about design thinking is as alternating periods of flare and focus, represented as a moving wave, expanding and contracting over time. Sometimes your job as a designer is to expand your thinking as widely as possible, to take in lots of new ideas and information, and to quickly imagine lots of different approaches and solutions. At other parts of the process, it's important to narrow

your thinking and address one particular challenge with one particular solution.

Design Thinking for Leading and Learning is an iterative cycle with six overlapping phases. During the Discover phase, designers explore and define a particular problem. The best designers remain open and take in all kinds of information from diverse sources through observations and interviews, and they try not to prejudge a problem before really understanding it. Then during the Focus phase, a designer uses all that information to narrow in on one specific facet of a problem to tackle. That's not meant to give up on wicked, complex problems, but rather to tackle them in a systematic, piecemeal way.

Nichole Pinkard is a professor at Northwestern University who has done incredible work studying and designing informal learning environments in the city of Chicago that have inspired educators around the world. She leads the Digital Youth Network, an organization that's designed to create learning opportunities and learning spaces that empower youth to develop the critical literacies that are going to be necessary to enable them to be active citizens. Professor Pinkard has a compelling description for why focusing on small, actionable steps can be a powerful way to get to bigger change:

> *When we're trying to decide what's going to be the next focus of our work, we really have to take a holistic view. And we've made mistakes in the past of focusing on the big solution. We'd say, "Let's look for a solution that's going to take us two years; it's going to be the mother of all solutions." ... So, we spent years, initially, trying to spend two years coding and say, here's our solution—those systems never worked. The systems that worked for us were the systems that we ended up with 100 iterations on,*

(Continued)

because we made small, incremental improvements. And at that point, your stakeholders are able to define what their needs are at that level. It's harder for them to define whole new paradigms, right? Five years ago, someone couldn't tell you what blended learning needed to be.... So, in that sense, it's really figuring out how to focus in on smaller milestones, and then to allow those milestones to combine together into bigger solutions.

In the MIT Teaching Systems Lab, we've had the same experience. One principle I often share with new students and staff is that the quality of whatever we are building is often directly related to how many iterations a product experiences. As Professor Pinkard observes, our best work goes through dozens of iterations of exploring, prototyping, evaluating, and refining before it comes into a final form that we're proud of.

Once you have successfully focused on some aspect of a problem, the scope of thinking expands again as designers enter the Imagine phase and begin brainstorming multiple solutions. In this phase, you try to rapidly imagine many possible solutions to your focal issue. From this long list of possibilities, designers will pick a solution to develop and narrow their focus again as they develop a prototype. Prototypes can be wildly diverse; it could be a storyboard or narrative of an experience or a fully developed part of a larger whole or a quick sketch of something that could be more sophisticated. For instance, when we prototype new software for mobile devices, we often just draw what screens might look like on a stack of index cards since drawing is often much faster and cheaper than coding and programming. We can learn a lot from people's initial reactions to a new idea before we put all the time and effort into realizing that ideal with more realistic designs.

Ideally, you will design a prototype that other people can try out as soon as possible. In the Try phase, designers put their prototypes in front of real people, ideally folks who resemble the end user as closely as possible. It's good to evaluate new ideas for a kindergarten class with other teachers, better still to evaluate them with other kindergarten teachers, and best of all to try them out with real kindergarten students.

Often a project will require many cycles of refining prototypes and trying them out again to iteratively refine a prototype. After a number of these cycles, sometimes many and sometimes just one, you'll feel like it's time to organize your thoughts and get feedback on what you've learned from these cycles of prototyping and playtesting. In the Reflect and Share phase, you pause the work of iterative design to organize your thoughts and get feedback from community members, stakeholders, and other designers.

In some cases, these cycles lead you to realize that your designs aren't working, and you need to go back and explore your problem and focal area again. Sometimes, you realize the real problem is just different from what you thought it was. Sometimes, after many cycles of iteration and refinement, what you design works great, and it simply gets integrated into your practice. It grows out of being an innovation and just becomes part of the routine of your classroom or school. Then you rest and celebrate and start dreaming up what your next innovation might be.

KEY PRINCIPLES TO DESIGN THINKING FOR LEADING AND LEARNING

Here are a few key principles to guide your understanding of Design Thinking for Leading and Learning.

Design thinking asks you to **assume a hopeful, optimistic stance** toward addressing challenges in our schools. Design approaches assume that we can find a better way forward, especially when we work together with our colleagues, students, community, and families. When conversations and discussions feel stuck, designing, prototyping, and making can be one way to get unstuck.

In early phases, our goal is to **make failure cheap**. It's totally normal for new ideas not to work. It's hard to get a really great design on the first try and much easier to get to something good on the 25th try. The only way to get to dozens of tries is to make each one—especially the early ones—small enough and light enough that you can learn something from a prototype without feeling like you are so invested in a particular new approach that you can't abandon it without a sense of doom.

One way to keep the costs of experimentation down is to **embrace a bias to action**. As you think through all the phases of Design Thinking for Leading and Learning, be careful not to get bogged down in the first half of the cycle: Discover, Focus, and Imagine. Put time limits on those activities, so you can get to Prototyping and Trying new things out. If your prototypes aren't working right, you can return to those earlier phases. There is a lot that you can learn from thinking and brainstorming with colleagues, but the fastest learning will be when you get small, minimum viable prototypes in front of people as soon as you can.

Use small steps to tackle big problems. In order to have a bias to action, you have to start with designs that are small enough to quickly try out. As you see that experiments are working, when your minimum prototypes prove to be viable, then you can build on the foundations of your small steps toward bigger and more comprehensive designs. This complements making failure cheap: when you iterate in small steps, the missteps don't feel so costly. Design thinking can help us change whole systems, but we usually tackle systems design by building up from smaller pieces.

Include diverse perspectives as you design. Nobody understands the challenges that your students and families face better than your students and families. Bringing in diverse perspectives to address important challenges means actively reaching out to make space for people who may feel marginalized or excluded from school or the community. An important starting point is simply finding ways for students to be involved in imagining what school could be. The late Bob Vieth worked for many years at MIT's Edgerton Center for engineering outreach and education, where he led professional development for educators. Bob asked:

> *The kids who are going to be in your classroom—do you ask for their input about how to design it? Most teachers will say no, because the teachers are used to having things just so in their classrooms. They want to know where things are. They want it to look neat. And I get all that. But the teacher is not the end user in the classroom. The kid is. So, shouldn't kids have some input as to what the classroom should look like? And it's a perfect challenge to be addressed by design thinking.*

Finally, **never lose sight of improving student learning**. In product design, it's usually good enough to get people to buy or use things. A special challenge for educators is that sometimes kids buy into activities that aren't that great for learning. Movie Day in class is rated very highly by students, but doesn't necessarily have the learning outcomes we're looking for. As you think about the later stages for Design Thinking for Leading and Learning, such as the Try and Reflect and Share phases, a crucial consideration will be not just whether young people enjoy and participate in a new activity, but whether it really leads to new learning and growth.

In the rest of this chapter, I walk through the six design phases. But before that, let me offer you an alternative pathway. There are some people when faced with new approaches and ideas who like to get the whole picture in their head before starting. If you are that kind of person—the kind of person who reads the manual before assembling the new Ikea furniture—then read on!

But if you really like to just dive right in, I have two additional resources for you. There are two online workbooks that are supplements to this book that you can find at www.wiley.com/go/iterate. The first workbook has a guided design exercise where you will develop a new morning routine, vacation trip, or party for a partner, family member, or friend. If you like to start a new exploration by diving right in, you might consider reading that section first and conducting the activities described there, and then coming back here and reading through these steps in greater detail. The second workbook will walk you through a design activity for improving your school or context.

SIX PHASES OF DESIGN THINKING FOR LEADING AND LEARNING

DISCOVER

Human-centered design starts by trying to deeply understand people's lived experiences. Often in schools, adults unilaterally decide what the problems are and what the solutions should be. In the wake of the pandemic, after many students had missed weeks of school, many schools and districts

offered extra summer school programs. The problem was missed school; the solution was more school in the summer. Simple, right? Unfortunately, uptake of these programs in the summer of 2021 was quite low in many places. Students and families weren't interested in summer school, or they weren't interested in the programs being offered.[10] There was a mismatch between what schools thought young people and families needed, and what families and students thought they needed.

The first phase of Design Thinking for Leading and Learning is Discover, where you will take a fresh look at your school or classroom with an open mind. Solving problems starts by understanding how your learners, families, and colleagues understand their problems and needs from their perspective. Understanding challenges from the perspectives of your stakeholders is essential to developing solutions that meet their real, felt needs, as opposed to the needs that we assume that people have. The goal of the Discover phase is to try to uncover something new about the people in your school, the challenges they face, and what might help them thrive. Other design frameworks refer to the Discover phase as the "Empathize" or "Understand" phase, which are also good terms.

Since human-centered design starts with people and their lived experiences, we need to give a name to the people who are the subjects of our inquiry—the people we serve. In the design community these folks are often called "users" or "end users." It's not my favorite term for education contexts. It makes more sense in software or product design, where the people will be "using" the end design. In education, we do much more than "use" schools—we live in them, participate in them, learn through them, and so forth. I've found it more helpful to talk in terms of "learners," "families," "educators," "community members," or even "stakeholders." But "users" is a term of art that I'll reference from time to time.

Starting with people helps us do several things. First, it helps us relax our assumptions about a situation and to try to understand a challenge or issue from multiple perspectives, especially perspectives different from our own. Second, it helps us understand problems as the people who live with them every day understand them. And third, starting with people gives us the opportunity to invite folks into the design process with us. In the next chapter, I introduce you to specific techniques for learning more about user needs, including conducting interviews and surveys.

Amos Winter is a professor of mechanical engineering at MIT, who works in the Global South on projects ranging from desalination and irrigation to wheelchairs, prosthetics, and mobility. He's an able-bodied White guy from MIT, trying to be of service in places and communities very different from his own upbringing and experience. In this interview excerpt, he talks about how important it is to build partnerships with community members:

> *You don't want to come in with the perspective of "I am designing for you." Instead, you want to come in with a perspective of "I'm designing with you. I want to know your knowledge about the problem. I want to know your constraints and requirements. I want to acknowledge the value of that knowledge in comparison to my knowledge. And I want to show you that together, by combining our knowledge, we can produce something better than either of us could have done alone." And just coming in with that perspective and mutual respect goes a long way in engaging an end user and getting honest feedback from them.... "You as an end user, you have as much or more valuable information than I do, even though I'm a trained engineer. You know about your life, you know about your problems, you know about your wants and needs." And I try to connect on that level.*

During the Discover phase, you will also examine the context and environment you're designing in by looking at *design constraints* and *design freedoms*. A design constraint is an aspect of the context you cannot change. For example, if you want to rethink transportation for your school district, you have no control over the roads between students' homes and your school buildings. In contrast, design freedoms are advantages present in the context that you can use in your design. In our example about redesigning school transportation, design freedoms might be a warm climate that allows walking and biking year-round, or public or private transportation options in the city.

In working with educators, my experience is that our profession can be a wee bit too focused on constraints. I would encourage you and your colleagues, as you are looking through the data you get back from Discover, to focus on design freedoms first. In the chapters ahead, we'll explore a specific tool called an Asset Map to help you think about all the tools and resources in your school that might help you be successful. Of course, constraints are real, and you will need to consider them, but the post-pandemic era is an interesting time to be reflecting on constraints. So much of schooling seemed rigid and fixed before the pandemic, and then schools implemented dramatic changes to many aspects of schooling to make remote and hybrid learning work. So many pieces of schools that seemed permanent proved to be malleable. I'd encourage you to bring that same spirit of open mindedness to your design work.

Put another way, don't dismiss the impossible. During the early parts of the pandemic, I worked with Boston Public School teacher Neema Avashia to interview students about their needs and desires during remote learning. One of her students said, "I wish I had a button that I could just press and a teacher would appear to help me."

This young woman's comment helped me reflect on one of the magical things about schools. If you are a young person, and you raise your hand—almost anywhere in a school: a classroom, the library, a cafeteria, and so forth—it's reasonably likely that soon an adult will come and check on you.[11]

It might be impossible for most school communities to design a button that magically summons a teacher. But Neema's student articulated an important need in a powerful way: she wanted to be able to get quick access to an educator when she got stuck. A magic button might not meet that need, but lots of feasible designs could: a Zoom room that always had a few teachers present ready to help and tutor, a text number that was monitored most hours by staff, or other ways for kids at a distance to get quick help from an adult getting unstuck.

But don't worry about solutions to any of this yet. In the Discover phase, when a student tells you she wants a button that magically summons a teacher, ask lots more follow-up questions. Which teachers? For what purpose? At what times? What would the button look like? How would you advertise it? Can you tell me more about what it feels like to be stuck? Try to understand as much as you can about how people understand their problems and worry about developing the magic of solutions later.

FOCUS

The next phase of the design process is "Focus," the stage where designers use what they have learned about people's needs, challenges, and life experiences to identify a particular problem to work on.

In the Discover phase, you learn a lot about the needs of the people you serve—specific and meaningful goals that are part of your stakeholders' lived experiences. These are lenses that you can use to frame a design problem, which is a challenge that can be addressed through a specific solution.

The basic outline of this stage is simple. Comb through your Discover data and start proposing problem areas to work on. One useful framing for a problem area is a "How might we . . ." question. A how-might-we question imagines addressing a user need without being overly prescriptive about a particular solution.

- How might we help remote students get fast access to support from educators?

- How might we create additional learning experiences for students who have many school absences?

- How might we get more formative feedback from students, without so many graded assignments that are a major source of stress for them?

- How might we increase the number of students with disabilities who are included in mainstream classes, without having teachers feel overwhelmed by the extra planning and differentiation?

The size and the scope of the problem that you tackle depends a little bit on how many colleagues are working with you and how much time and how many resources you have. It can be a good idea to start by working on something that feels more focused, tightly bound, and tractable. If you can find success solving small, narrower problems, then you can build on those successes to broader challenges.

The ways that designers frame the problem can powerfully influence the spaces that we explore for solutions. For instance, in learning design we often think about our most "typical" students and what resources and experiences they would need to be successful. It makes sense to think about typical students; there are a lot of them. But it can be quite powerful to frame our problems around students who are atypical; when we design for the margins, we often find ways of supporting people with distinct strengths and needs that also help more "typical" students. Jos Boys leads the Disordinary Architecture Project, an initiative to center disability in urban design. She argues that designing for variation rather than the typical can be a powerful starting point for design:

> *This means challenging assumptions of normalcy in our everyday routines and space; and investigating what kinds of bodies are imagined and operationalized in building and urban design, so as to reimagine these differently; and as a means of generating new kinds of design investigations and practices. By starting from difference—from mis-fitting, unruly and non-conforming bodies—dis/ability becomes a creative generator, producing new, previously unnoticed ways into designing.* [12]

Educators working on universal design for learning (UDL) have reached similar conclusions in learning design. When designers start tackling problems by centering the needs of language learners and folks with dyslexia, attention disorders, vision impairment, and other disabilities, they end up building learning resources with embedded supports like voice-to-text or large font options that specifically meet the needs of particular learners but end up being useful in varying degrees to all learners.

In choosing a focus area, one tension that you will constantly encounter is balancing between areas that are small enough to see immediate change while also wanting to navigate toward bigger, more systemic improvements. Good design always involves reconciling these kinds of tensions. Jason Lee is a former design director at Agncy, a Boston-based design firm that works with schools and non-profit organizations to address challenges through human-centered design. Jason talked in compelling ways about these challenges:

> As human-centered designers, we take an innately people-centered view of the world, right? We want to empathize with the needs of the individuals we're designing for. On the other hand, when you're dealing with something as complex as urban education, there are times when the needs of the system need to mesh with the needs of the individual. Especially when you're talking about a large, urban school district where issues like equity and fairness and creating education for some of our neediest people are the essential questions of the work that this district is doing. Being able to hold that tension in your head between "What do we need to do as a system to be equitable?" and "What are the individual needs of the 56,000, 57,000 families across the system?"—that's the sort of hairy ball that we're always trying to untangle.
>
> Systems are just made up of people. Everybody who works here is actually gunning for the same goal. They all want the same thing, which is quality education for children in this city. The challenges arise because systems have a lot of legacy components to them, which come from previous eras where values may not have to do both—improve legacy components and build new values—at the same time.

If you find that the focus area you choose feels too narrow or too small in the face of the big challenges that schools face, you might be tempted to try to attack a problem through a much bigger or more ambitious frame. If you have a lot of community support—a lot of support for families, teachers, school leaders, and school board members—that can be a great strategy. But if you are just getting started, consider starting your design work by tackling problems that feel actionable and immediate while making a commitment to spiral the work up toward more ambitious change.

In the next chapter, we go over specific strategies for how to go from observable data to underlying challenges and how to keep our design problems tightly-scoped and actionable.

IMAGINE

After you've identified an area of focus, the next step is to imagine a wide range of possible solutions and approaches. This can be a bit of a whiplash moment for new designers. As I've mentioned before, good design alternates between periods of flare and focus, between exploring new ideas widely and then focusing on particular approaches. You've  just gone through a focusing process to identify a problem or opportunity area. Now it's time to flare back out and to imagine a wide range of potential solutions to the challenge.

Kevin Robinson worked as a designer and software developer for several years in the MIT Teaching Systems Lab. He had an unusual background; he was a teacher of students with special needs, then a software engineer at Twitter, then worked with me at MIT for several years before moving on to work for a while with a local public school district, and then back to engineering with Google Research. Here's how Kevin described the Imagine phase of Design Thinking for Leading and Learning:

At the Imagine stage of the design process, you have a pretty clear idea of what problem you're solving and who you're serving. But you don't yet know how you're going to solve it and how you're going to help them. So, what you want to do is create a wide range of possibilities and really explore the whole space of ways you could help this person or group. You want to do that widely and broadly and not limit yourself to one particular solution upfront. Imagine is one of the most fun and energizing parts of the design process. You're taking all of these possibilities and throwing them out with people, and it feels really exciting often. But it can be challenging, too, especially when you're trying to come up with ideas from scratch or you're trying to figure out— how do we meet the aspirations that we have of solving this problem and serving these people?

A crucial part of brainstorming in the Imagine phase is making space for ideas that are half-baked or not obviously useful. When we critique or reject ideas too early in the process, it leads to two kinds of problems. First, sometimes powerful ideas come at problems sideways or through other unexpected approaches. There really are ideas "so crazy that they just might work." Also, the source of most good ideas is not an extraordinary moment of inspiration, but iterating over bad ideas to make them okay, then iterating over okay ideas to make them good. Second, we don't want people self-censoring their ideas as we are imagining new possibilities. Even when ideas seem pretty bonkers or wrong-headed, it's usually worth letting them get some airtime and space. Here's Kevin again on pushing through when ideas seem a little off:

> *One thing that's really powerful is not judging your ideas too soon, letting yourself be comfortable with the fact that you don't have really good ideas immediately, and just sticking at it, focusing on the problem, and coming up with other possibilities. There's going to be those moments where you think, "I've sort of exhausted everything. There's no other ideas here." Stay with that and see if you can come up with other ideas. There's also going to be moments where like, "I just thought of a new idea. Oh, that's a terrible idea." And just let that pass, continue on. Come up with other bad ideas. The more bad ideas you come up with, the more bad ideas you can shape into good ideas. A common mistake during ideation is anchoring too specifically on one possible solution.*

As Kevin says, a key part of the Imagine phase is generating lots of ideas, finding the connections between them, and seeing how they cluster around themes and approaches. Making people feel comfortable sharing their ideas is crucial to getting good volume and velocity of imagination. There is, however, at least one place where I might intervene in brainstorming if I thought folks were getting off track. When people start organizing their imagination around deficit views of students, families, or colleagues, I might step in to ask folks to assume good intentions, especially of marginalized people in the community. It's rarely helpful to imagine our partners in learning as recalcitrant, and better instead to focus on how systems can better meet people's needs for engagement, connection, and commitment.

PROTOTYPE

I love prototyping. It's the place where new ideas come to life for the first time. Your challenge when prototyping is to get a kernel of an idea out of your head and into the physical world, where other people can see, touch, and interact with the earliest renderings of your imagined solution.

There are two key principles for prototyping: build it fast and get it in front of people. When we design solutions to problems, we are at great risk of being trapped by our biases and assumptions. When we make physical representations of new ideas and get them in front of the people we hope to serve, we create opportunities for other people to challenge our assumptions, to help us see old problems with fresh eyes, and to point the way to solutions that meet the real, felt need of people on the ground. The heart of prototyping is quickly moving through iterative cycles of generating low-fidelity prototypes, getting feedback in the Try phase, and then making slightly higher-fidelity prototypes as ideas become validated and refined by people in your community.

When the Teaching Systems Lab was just getting started, we had the good fortune to hire Yasmine Kotturi, now a postdoc at the Human-Computer Interaction Institute at Carnegie Mellon University, who is a true prototyping aficionado. Her doctoral work examines how entrepreneurs from minoritized backgrounds can find support and support each other in community makerspaces. For Yasmine, prototyping isn't just a way of making stuff, but a way of engaging people:

Prototyping, to me, is a communication style. It's really this way of taking all the amazing ideas that we have in our head and putting them out into the world to be able to share them with other people and get feedback on them. And I think the key insight with prototyping is that it's very cheap. It's very fast and easy. And although it's simple, that doesn't mean it's any less valuable. Use prototyping as a way to share your ideas with the people around you. And not only does this allow them to get feedback and to see what it is that you have inside your head, but also to be able to then take it the next step forward to making your solution concrete.

An ongoing challenge in Design Thinking for Leading and Learning is figuring out when to move from one stage to the next. Here's Yasmine again:

One question I often am asked by students is, When should we move from the imagine stage to the prototyping stage? And the answer is often earlier than you feel comfortable doing. For some reason we feel very uncomfortable with taking all the awesome ideas that we have in our head and putting them out into the physical world, because they can seem awkward and may not seem like a refined idea. But definitely earlier than you think.

Don't think of prototyping as the step that happens after you've come up with a good idea worth building. Instead, think of prototyping as the way to figure out what's worth building. You start with simple, lightweight prototypes, and move your way to more complex, solid designs. If all your prototype ideas flop, you can always step back in the cycle and do more focusing or imagining. The goal of prototyping is to get ideas out of your head and into the world where other people can interact with them.

In the late 2010s at MIT, our faculty and leaders realized that we had some real issues with student well-being, particularly for our freshman. Our students were brilliant and talented, passionate about science and engineering, and surrounded by resources and laboratories where they could pursue their interests. Surveys also showed that they were much sadder, stressed, and overwhelmed than students at peer institutions, and that these negative feelings were most concentrated among our LGBTQ and underrepresented minority students. As an institution, we decided we need to revisit the first-year experience and figure out how we could maintain a rigorous introduction to MIT while helping students preserve more of their sense of self, fun, and happiness.

To the credit of MIT leadership, one of the signature components of this reform effort was a generously-staffed new course for students called *Designing the First-Year Experience*, which I helped to teach along with faculty from Aero/Astro, Mechanical Engineering, and the School of Management—departments that all had a strong tradition of design. We had undergraduate and graduate students from diverse backgrounds, representing schools and programs across the university, come together for a semester of studying at MIT and peer institutions, interviewing key stakeholders, and designing new approaches to the freshman year. Our students played a crucial role in leading this important reform.

Now, obviously, you can't "prototype" an entire year-long experience for 1,000 undergraduates during a 15-week fall course, at least in the sense that you can't have people do various versions of their entire freshman year a few different times to tell us what worked and didn't. So, in this context of experience design, we had our student teams prototype particular elements of the first-year experience or representations of particular elements. For specific key parts of the first-year experience, like the orientation activity fair, we could develop simulations of the experience that other students could try out. For components that extend over longer time periods, like a course schedule, we could have students look at sample weekly schedules or example transcripts and have them give their feedback on those specific artifacts that are representative components of longer programs. When prototyping long and complex experiences, a useful strategy is to imagine key moments in that longer sequence of experience and develop prototypes for those key moments.

There are as many ways to prototype as there are ways to interact with the world: sketching and storyboarding, paper prototyping and wireframing, and physical prototyping and rehearsals. With each round of prototyping, we hope to generate increasingly high-fidelity prototypes. Typically, it's helpful to start with the simplest, cheapest, quickest form, like sketches of new ideas or storyboards that create quick narratives of an experience. In the Teaching Systems Lab, when we consider building a new piece of mobile software, we often don't start with programming and code. Programming is hard and takes a long time! But it's quite easy to draw a mobile phone outline on an index card, and then draw what a screen interface might look like. Then we draw 5 or 10 more screens that highlight different buttons, menus, or steps in an experience. In early tryouts, we might have people "click" on an index card that shows one screen, and then narrate to them what happens and show them the next index card with the next screen that might appear. With these index cards, we can "program," deploy, and test new software ideas in minutes. I share more specific approaches to prototyping in the next chapter.

The whole purpose of prototyping is getting feedback from others, which is the focus of the next stage of Design Thinking for Leading and Learning.

TRY

Most design thinking representations call this stage the "Test" stage. From our extensive user research, we found that a lot of young people don't have particularly positive associations with the word "test." We use Try as an alternative. In our lab, we don't think of prototypes as assessments that we pass or fail; instead, we try out our prototypes with community members to understand what's working, what's falling short, and how we can improve.

As soon as you have prototypes, you should be having other people try them out. Just as Yasmine argued that you should move from Imagining to Prototyping earlier than your intuition will suggest, the same is true for tryouts. Don't think of tryouts as a way to figure out if a refined prototype is good or working; tryouts are the mechanism by which prototypes become good.

Andrew Sutherland is the entrepreneur who founded Quizlet, the flashcard app that's widely used in schools around the world. He started a degree at MIT, but left before graduating to focus on Quizlet. Design at Quizlet is organized around sprints, periods of two to three weeks during which user experience designers, instructional experts, and software engineers work on some new feature or approach. When teams develop an idea for a new sprint, one of the first project management steps is to schedule a "playtest" in a real classroom at the end of the sprint. A playtest is a structure—a field visit, an event, a meeting—that lets designers observe users interacting with a prototype. Long before the idea for a new feature or approach gets fully formed, design teams know that they need to have something ready to put in front of real teachers and students. Deadlines concentrate the mind!

In a school context, you might think about what ongoing meetings you have that could be converted to playtests. What grade-level team meetings, department meetings, professional learning community (PLC) meetings, or faculty meetings could be reserved for design teams to share and try out their prototypes? Could you form a student Curriculum Club, a group that's willing to meet regularly to discuss school improvement and give feedback on new designs? Does the student government or Parent-Teacher Association or school board have meeting times that they would be willing to devote to engaging with prototypes? It may seem a bit crazy to have school board members involved in playtesting, since they are primarily concerned with high-level school policy, but one of the best ways to have board members be well informed in making school policy is to help them get insight into the nitty-gritty details of teaching, learning, and school life.

Healthy cycles of prototyping and tryouts are tight and iterative; people feel urgency about getting new designs created and getting feedback from community members. Scheduling playtest events well in advance of when they are needed can create productive deadlines and ensure that you have time to gather the best people for trying new ideas out. As prototypes get to be higher and higher fidelity, more design time may be required between periods of testing, but in most stages of design, prototyping and tryouts should feel like they are regular parts of a design team's work.

One key step for preparing for tryouts is to articulate your *design hypothesis*. Every prototype embodies a design hypothesis, a belief about how a new approach to design could lead to new feelings or behaviors among your users. However, as designers, sometimes those hypotheses are tacit or unclear. When our students in *Designing the First-Year Experience* course developed ideas for a new activity fair or new credit requirements, one of our jobs as instructors was to ask them, before tryouts, to articulate exactly how their new designs would lead to better interactions and better experiences than their previous designs. Once they could clearly articulate their design hypotheses, they could then review their testing protocols—the steps they outlined to have users play through their prototypes—to see what kind of data they needed to collect to disconfirm or confirm their hypotheses.

As you collect evidence from your tryouts, you will have new information and insight that can lead you to different places in the cycle of Design Thinking for Leading and Learning. Sometimes users love elements of your prototype, and you go back into the prototyping process to refine your prototype. But early on, that's not always the case. Maybe you need to go back and Imagine new solutions and prototype something else. Or maybe you discover that you don't understand your stakeholder's problems as well as you thought, and you need to go back to Discover or Focus. Each tryout leads you to a new cycle, and the more cycles of discovery, prototyping, and tryouts, the closer you will be to new designs and experiences that serve your students, colleagues, and families.

REFLECT AND SHARE

In Design Thinking for Leading and Learning, we call the final stage Reflect and Share. As with every previous stage, it's a bit of a misnomer to call this the "final" stage, when as a designer you will be reflecting and sharing throughout the whole process. Mitchel Resnick is a faculty member at MIT and the head of the Lifelong Kindergarten Lab, responsible for the Scratch programming community and many other great learning inno- vations. Professor Resnick empha- sizes that one of the crucial purposes of concluding reflection is to draw

generalizable principles from specific experiences. When we reflect dur- ing design, it's to fix a problem within the design. When we reflect after design, it's usually to learn something for future work. Here's Mitch:

A colleague of mine, Edith Ackermann, often talks about a dance of diving into the design and then stepping back and reflect- ing. And I think that the best way for students to learn about the design process is to experience it, but then to reflect upon their experience and to learn about the process through their reflections on the experiences that they've had. So, this dance of diving in and stepping back, it happens over and over. You're constantly thinking about what's going on to get a better under- standing to help you in the design process.

I think the reflection is where you turn the concrete ac- tivity into more general observations that you can apply to oth- er things that you do. As people are reflecting on their work, one problem can be that they get caught up in the details, because you reflect upon how this particular thing fit into that particular thing and go through step by step of each particular thing you did, without stepping back and thinking about the significance of this—of Why did this go wrong? You might just say, What went

> *wrong? But not Why did it go wrong? Or what you ended up do-*
> *ing, but not why you ended up doing it. So, I think making sure*
> *that in reflecting, it's not just capturing the specific things you*
> *did, but stepping back and thinking about the motivations and*
> *the lessons learned from what you did.*

As all teachers know, one of the best ways to cement your under-standing of new ideas is to explain them to someone else. Sharing the fruits of your design and reflection not only lets you spread good ideas, but it helps you refine your best thinking from the project.

As your design shifts from prototyping and testing to imple-mentation, there are three good groups of stakeholders to reflect and share with: the design team itself, immediate community stakehold-ers, and wider communities in the field of education. Design teams can get together and talk about the process of design: what worked, what didn't, what could be improved for next time. Designers can talk with their community stakeholders and share evidence about how new practices are working and how they will be maintained or refined. Finally, designers can talk with wider communities in educa-tion, sharing their work across the district, or in disciplinary confer-ences or with other groups in education.

There are lots of benefits from sharing in more formal settings, like faculty meetings and conferences, but don't underestimate the benefits of more modest, informal opportunities to share your learn-ing as well. In the online courses that my lab has offered about design, we often assigned work where participants needed to complete some design activity and then share their results with one other person: a colleague, friend, or student. These informal conversations can create space for you to sharpen and refine your thinking for new projects, and they build solidarity with potential collaborators for future design projects. If your work is student facing, it's always valuable to debrief your efforts with students, both those directly affected by a new initiative and others who might be able to provide a fresh student perspective. Too often, school feels like something done *to* students, and Design Thinking for Leading and Learning creates opportunities for school to feel like something done *with* students.

REFLECTION AND INCLUSION

Reflection plays a crucial role throughout design, and I suggest two questions that should always be at the forefront of your thinking. First, who is invited to participate in this design? As mentioned earlier in the chapter, disability rights' advocates coined the phrase "Nothing about us without us" to demand that people with disabilities be at the table in conversations of policy, design, accommodation, and regulation. How can you work to involve the people most affected by your work into the process of design? Of course, it's the job of educators to make schools work, and it's the job of kids to roll in the mud, do schoolwork, play games, and watch for rainbows. Even if youth aren't in a position to lead and drive every phase of design, it's always worth reflecting on how and where they can be involved.

Second, how will your designs affect people from different backgrounds and life circumstances differently? How will they affect families with high school engagement differently than families with lower school engagement? How will it affect students who are thriving differently than students who are struggling? How will it play out differently along lines of gender, race, or affluence? Attending to these questions is one way to maintain an ongoing dialogue in design teams about who benefits from work and investments.

CONCLUSION

Amelia Peterson is one of the founding faculty members at the London Interdisciplinary School, a new university in the UK founded in 2020. She has a nice description of a design process called Spirals of Inquiry[13] (many similar things have different names, but don't let it distract you!), which offers a helpful summary of what this whole process looks like together:

> [Spirals of Inquiry] starts by asking students questions about how they're experiencing schools. One of the questions is, Can you name two adults in this school who think that you can be successful? And it's actually a really interesting, sort of telling question when teachers are confronted by the perspective of their students and how their students are experiencing the school environment. So, we see that as a really interesting specific example of the empathy stage of design thinking, where teachers are coming to understand their students' experience of the school and how they see how teachers feel about them. And then the next stage of the spiral would be to sort of go through this whole scanning process, understand how all the students are experiencing school, and then to identify a change that you, as a teacher, can make to improve how your students are experiencing their learning. And so that's kind of the stage where you're honing in on a problem, on a challenge that is going to become your design challenge, and you're going to make some improvement. So, you decide on the change you can make, and then you're implementing that, and you're going to be iterating on it. You're going to be improving it, tweaking it as you go

(Continued)

> *along. And the way that you would do that is really by look-*
> *ing for the impact that your change has had on your students.*
> *So, then you need to be going out, looking for evidence of the*
> *change, looking for what's going on for the students, maybe car-*
> *rying out that scanning process again in terms of asking them*
> *how that's changed, and then just continually working through*
> *that cycle. And that's why it's known as a spiral, because it just*
> *iterates round and round.*

Starting from simple questions such as "Who are two adults in this school who care about you?" is one way to spark an inquiry that can lead to cycles of design. During the worst of the COVID-19 pandemic, my colleagues Jal Mehta at the Harvard Graduate School of Education and Neema Avashia in the Boston Public Schools came up with five questions to help spark teacher reflection and improvement: What were the best parts of remote learning? What do you hope schools stop doing once remote learning ends? What was the hardest part of the past year? What are you most proud of? What do you hope adults in your school will do differently when we return from remote learning? These questions of discovery can lead to areas of focus, imaging solutions, and prototyping and testing those ideas.

Of course, there is no better way to get a feel for design thinking than to dive right in. In the next chapter, I share a few different ways for you to start or rev up your practice with Design Thinking for Leading and Learning.

GETTING STARTED WITH DESIGN

Now that you have an orientation to design thinking, I have three pathways for you to develop more practical knowledge with technique. In this chapter, I share some specific techniques for each of the six phases of Design Thinking for Leading and Learning. There are also two workbook chapters to this book, which offer two complete "walkthroughs" of design activities. The first is what I call a "starter" design exercise, where you work in a personal context, outside the education system, to do a full design cycle working on a problem like helping someone improve their morning routine or plan a trip or event. This exercise is fun and relatively quick, and it will expose you to a variety of design approaches quickly. The second walkthrough will guide you and a small group of colleagues through a school-based design exercise focused on improving some element of student learning. If you want to keep expanding your toolkit of design strategies, read on. When you are ready to dive in and start the work, you can use the two walkthrough workbooks, found at www.wiley.com/go/iterate as a guide.

DISCOVER

RESEARCH TO DISCOVER: SURVEYS, INTERVIEWS, AND OBSERVATIONS

Designing with people starts by listening closely to their experiences. Surveys, interviews, and observations are three important tools for discovering more about the people in your learning environment. There are zillions of great ways to use these methods, but three useful guidelines apply to all of them.

First, embrace the discipline of **holding back your assumptions and judgments**. When you talk to people or observe them, be curious about their answers and avoid leaping to your own interpretations or possible solutions. It's almost impossible to do this reliably, so a good note-taking strategy is to write down all the things you see and hear in one column, and then write down your impressions and assumptions in a second column. Try to focus more on writing in the first column during an interview or observation, and filling out the second column afterwards. In order to see the world through other people's eyes, we need to practice quieting our own assumptions and judgments.

Second, **be deliberate about engaging with people who are harder to reach**. If you send around a home survey in English, you won't learn from all the families who don't speak English. If you put out an open call for volunteers for a focus group, you won't get the people who don't like to volunteer. Actively seek out people on the margins to understand their experiences.

Third, try to **start your inquiry in an open-ended place**, before getting to more specific questions. As Amos Winter, the MIT mechanical engineering professor introduced in the previous chapter, says, "If you're going to conduct an interview, you want to go in with as few preconceptions as possible. You don't want to lead people to an answer. You want to ask them questions about their life and get their perspective." If you were in a school or district considering launching extra summer school to address absences or missed learning, it's not necessarily wrong to ask people what they think about summer school. But before you plant that idea in their head, ask them broader, more open-ended questions about their experiences and perceptions. How is school going? What have you or your students been learning? How do you feel about school? What would the ideal summer look like for you? Eventually, you might get to asking about summer school, but start with questions that let people talk about what's top of mind for them, not for you.

As you interview and survey people, one challenge is that they will tell you about their needs and desires, but they probably won't tell you exactly what to build or how. Here's Professor Winter again describing how to think about the answers that people give you:

I look at the design process as being similar to operating like a detective in that I'm always looking for clues behind what are requirements for a design and what are constraints. I think the best analogy to a clue is a latent need. When somebody is telling you about a problem in their life but not articulating a solution, and you have to extract from what they're saying what is their problem that I have to satisfy. The classic example is when Henry Ford started designing cars. He said, "if I asked people what they wanted, they would have said faster horses." Because people's context of travel was around horses. But that latent need they were expressing was: "I want to go from point A to point B faster." So, you don't necessarily have to use a horse to do that. You could use another device, which became the car.

I've done a lot of work on wheelchair designs, and I've done particularly a lot of work on wheelchairs for rural areas of developing countries. And nobody ever said to me, I want a wheelchair that goes fast and efficiently on rough terrain, that's small enough to use indoors, that's repairable in a village area, and that's low cost. What I heard instead was, "boy, it's really hard to get from my house to my job" or "jeez, my outdoor wheelchair doesn't fit in my home." And you get a sense of these latent needs which aren't directly expressed but are very important. And if you can get some insight into those needs, you can incorporate them into your design.

ITERATING ON DISCOVERY

I've described Design Thinking for Leading and Learning as a cycle with six phases, but really any of the phases can become iterative cycles themselves. With feedback and refinement, you can make your survey questions more useful, your interview questions more probing, and your observation notes more revealing.

The city of Boston has an internal design group called the Office of New Urban Mechanics with a mission to bring new design approaches to age-old municipal challenges. The office has an Education Lab, devoted to improving learning throughout the city. In 2016, as the group was starting, one of their first "internal clients" was the Food and Nutrition services group in the Boston Public Schools. Jaclyn Youngblood is a designer in that office, and she talks about starting a survey, getting 100 responses, and using those first responses to see if the survey was working to get the information they needed.

We want to continue to raise the bar on the quality of food, and the experience of being in a cafeteria. So, we worked with the administration at the school, worked with food and nutrition services, talked to the kitchen managers to say "hey, we're just going to come. We just want to observe and see what your lunch logistics look like. And we would love to ask your students what they like and don't about mealtime at school." And if they could change the physical space in some way, how might they want to change it?

And so, we ended up getting over 100 student responses through visiting various schools, which was the beginning of a database to say, okay, how might we turn this into something that is scalable, or did we ask the right questions? How did students react to us asking them these questions? Did they want to tell us more? Were they confusing questions?

Before getting too deep in the Discovery process on a big, district-wide investigation, the Education Lab team took the step of doing a round of iteration on their Discovery tools, to make sure they were finding what they were looking for. As a designer, Jaclyn Youngblood had a different background from the educators that she worked with, but she also recognized that while design language might be new to teachers, the ideas are very familiar:

Some of the language of design might be new for educators. But I think educators have been doing this forever. They always think about who is their audience, how do you tailor the message to the audience, how do you really empathize with the person or people sitting in front of you and make sure that what you're doing is meeting their needs? I think that's been a hallmark of education for a long time. And we're just trying to equip people with new tools and new language and a new approach that they can use in complement with the other things that they're already doing to think about issues in education or problems in education in just a slightly reframed way.

COMBINING LOCAL KNOWLEDGE WITH EDUCATION RESEARCH

Design often involves balancing tensions. Thus far, I've presented the essence of the Discover phase as conducting local research and understanding the people in your own context. That local knowledge is important, but it's not the only way to approach understanding problems. One reason we chose the term "Discover" over something like "Empathize" is that in our view, connecting with people isn't the only way to understand a problem space. People have been running schools for centuries, and they have been helping young people learn in structured ways for millennia. Humanity has learned a lot about schooling and learning in that time! It's important to balance the information you gain from talking to people in your context and learning about their experience with what you read in research and experience reports from other schools and learning environments to see how they approach problems similar to yours.

I would encourage you to be skeptical of thinking that overemphasizes "best practices," especially any approach that assumes that you can take things that work in one context and "scale them up" in lots of other places. Human-centered design is a good alternative to that kind of thinking, which deeply values what the people in your place and context know about their experiences and your shared school.

Human-centered design can also be informed by expertise and research from other places. Don't believe that best practices from another place will automatically work in yours, but don't discard them either. Don't ignore all the wisdom and insight that's in your community, but don't ignore everything you've learned in other schools either.

For instance, let's say that you work in a majority White school, with a majority White faculty, and you are working on a project to improve the experiences and learning of your Black and other minority students. Of course, it will be vital to talk with Black students and families about their experiences, the biggest frustrations and challenges they have with schools, and their ideas about how to make school more welcoming and more supportive of learning. At the same time, you will not be the first school working on this issue. There are many brilliant Black educators and researchers who have thought deeply and practiced extensively to address these challenges. (I can't help but to recommend *Start Where You Are But Don't Stay There* by my colleague Rich Milner.[1])

FOCUS

In the previous chapter, I talked about the "How might we . . ." statement as a useful way of framing a problem area. In this chapter, I share techniques for getting the concise "How might we . . ." statement from what you learned in the Discover phase.

GOING FROM OBSERVABLE DATA TO UNDERLYING CHALLENGES

Blade Kotelly is a senior lecturer at MIT in our Gordon Engineering Leadership Program, and he's a design consultant who has worked with companies like Sonos, the home speaker company, and Jibo, a firm that makes social robots. When we talked to Blade about the Focus phase, he emphasized the importance of using questions to get from the raw data of the Discover phase to some areas that would be good to work on in the Focus phase.

> *Finding really good opportunities to help users can be really challenging. And I think that's probably the thing you spend the most amount of time on to do it right and to find really good areas to attack. If it's about how they get to work, it's understanding why they get to work, and what they value as they get to work, and what they're concerned about as they get to work. And understanding their human emotions around that. And from there, it's trying to figure out what questions do you need*

to ask to figure out about the space... And they may not be even specific questions to ask a user but ask yourself as a designer. And then as you start to answer those questions, you begin to divine out where the interesting places are to start.

A great technique is using the "Five Whys" process where you can see any activity that the user is doing and try to ask why they are doing that. And as you keep asking why they are doing that thing that led to that first activity and go back and back, you get closer to understanding their human needs. Trying to do that can be really challenging. And it requires some practice. But the more you do it, the better you get. And soon you'll be able to understand really what's motivating someone and how to use different questions to inspire different thinking.

The activity is called Five Whys because the designer tries to ask these why questions five times, each time getting closer to the root causes of the issue. When you use processes like the Five Whys to do a root cause analysis, you might discover that the way that you initially framed your problem is quite different from the underlying causes. For instance, Agncy executive director Augusta Meill talked about how, in her work with the Boston Public Schools, the underlying challenges were as much emotional as they were logistical and procedural.

So, we started by doing in-depth research at the central office level. We learned from the superintendent and his executive team, through to some of the departments that make the central office tick, to understand how does this district operate from the top down? What are its values and aspirations and

(Continued)

strategies? And then we have been moving down across the layers of the system. So, we just spent about six weeks conducting similar ethnographies in schools, doing shadows of principals, sitting in classrooms with teachers, sitting in the cafeteria and eating lunch with students, and conducting that human-centered research, but at multiple altitudes across this system.

Some of the findings that we reported back to the district are around a real sense of isolation that exists at every level, from the central office folks who feel very removed from the on-the-ground work—all the way through to families who can feel very disconnected from the educational machine that their children are participating in—to teachers who will say things like, I go in my classroom at 8:30, I close the door, and then it's just me and the kids. And that sense of isolation in its worst case can result in, sometimes, competition within the system, which is really detrimental to doing this broad, transformative work at scale.

Boston Public Schools didn't hire Agncy to work on their "isolation problem," they hired them to address organizational issues, and the roots of those issues emerged through discovery. The kinds of things that trigger districts to do a deep dive into problems are usually much more immediate concerns: declining test scores, attendance, or graduation rates, or increases in teacher turnover, student conflict, or parent expressions of concern. Sometimes a focused investigation reveals that superficial problems that appear different on the surface can have shared underlying causes. When Agncy discovered that a sense of isolation appeared to be a core underlying problem across the district, they could frame that as a set of how-might-we statements, like "How might we make the work of teachers more collaborative and joyful?" or "How might we make students and families feel more connected to the district as a whole community, not just the parts of school they regularly encounter?" Those kinds of focus areas can create new space to imagine possible solutions.

FINALIZING A FOCUS AREA

A common way to proceed through the Focus phase with a group is to have a team of people collect a series of "How might we . . ." statements or similar problem statements on a board somewhere, and then have folks decide which of those statements should be the problem area to focus on.

This can be one of the most fraught moments of the design process. You've spent a whole bunch of time flaring out and trying to understand different perspectives on different problems, and now you are hoping a team will come together and work on one specific area of focus. Choosing one area of focus necessarily means setting aside a lot of the other good ideas that you've generated.

Sometimes it proves not to be a problem, and you can generate consensus around one idea that seems quite urgent. But it is not uncommon that groups struggle to agree on where they should focus limited time and effort together.

I have two suggestions for these challenges. First, if you get stuck deciding where to focus, go back to your key stakeholders: students, families, and colleagues. What do they identify as most important? Many times, when you are stuck in design work in schools, young people are your best asset in finding the way forward. I'm highlighting this point here in the Focus area, but it's true in every stage. When you are having trouble finding your way in school improvement, turn to the wisdom and experience of young people.

Another approach is to try to reduce the stakes of the decision by creating design cycles that are small enough to allow for multiple tries and multiple iterations. Consider taking on a first area with a focused problem and a tightly bound minimum viable prototype. When a design cycle is small and light, if it fails, you can discard it and try another approach. If it's successful, that gives you a chance to try to draw in and build excitement with more reluctant partners. It's natural for people to have a hard time letting go of their ideas. If people know there is a realistic chance of coming back to an idea, they are more likely to be willing to say goodbye for a while.

IMAGINE

After you've identified an area of focus, the next step is to imagine a wide range of possible solutions and approaches. The goal here is to flip again from focus to flare, and here are some strategies for rapidly generating lots of possible design ideas.

There is extensive research into brainstorming, and one finding stands out above all others: start brainstorming individually; refine and assess ideas together. Every group has power dynamics, and these power dynamics will inevitably influence your design process. Loud people, confident people, well-established people, and people with conventional markers of power and privilege will overshadow other voices. One way to protect fragile new ideas is to let people start their brainstorming individually and bring lots of ideas to the table, ideally with only limited connection to their origins. The ubiquitous Post-it Note is a pretty good tool for this: instead of having people shout out new ideas with one person writing them down, have individuals write down their ideas and put them in some public, shared space where they can be considered at a distance from the person who generated the idea.[2]

Eventually, you will need the shared genius of your whole team to sort through these ideas, riff on them, expand them, and refine them, and it's impossible to avoid the effects of power dynamics throughout that whole process (though of course you should be constantly trying to elevate and protect the voices of the least powerful and most marginal in your design process). But that initial phase of imagining is particularly fraught and vulnerable to people critiquing new ideas and pathways too early. So, whenever you can, brainstorm individually first, and then sift through ideas together.

As with every phase of the design cycle, I encourage you to constantly ask yourself who is in the room and whose ideas have a chance to come to the surface. It can be important to include people who have valuable perspectives, but not enough time to be involved in an entire design cycle. Consider how community members can participate in certain phases of design, such as generating new ideas or selecting ideas to move forward with prototyping. As you move from stage to stage in Design Thinking for Leading and Learning, ask yourself how you can create more spaces for diverse voices to contribute.

USER PERSONAS (OR COMMUNITY PERSONAS)

One useful tool for this stage of Design Thinking for Leading and Learning is a set of user personas (which you can call community personas if you want to avoid the term "user"). To develop a set of user personas, ask each person on your design team to brainstorm three or four different stakeholders who will be engaging with your problem and solution. Ideally, these personas emerge from distinctive individuals or interesting composites of people who you have met during your Discover work.

When I facilitate this exercise, I like to give people a template for drawing a persona on a blank sheet of paper broken up into four quadrants. In the top left, I encourage people to give the user a name, some basic demographic data, and a sketch of what they might look like. The other three quadrants will vary from project to project, but generally I encourage people to list a persona's most urgent goals and needs, their likes and dislikes, and their stances toward a context (school, peers, a specific class, etc.) or a problem of practice (signing up for classes, notetaking, scheduling a meeting with a teacher, etc.).

With these specific personas, your design team can have conversations throughout the design process about how each persona might see a particular phase of the design process. How would each persona describe the problem area? How would each persona rate a set of potential solutions? Of course, the best way to get diverse perspectives on a design process is to have all those perspectives constantly in the room or regularly engaged in providing feedback. But it's your job to make school better, not the full-time job of parents, or students, or community members, so when you can't have people together for every stage, personas can be a powerful way to keep different voices in your design space and process.

IMAGINE BY ANALOGY

T.S. Eliot wrote that "Immature poets imitate; mature poets steal." People have been educating youth for millennia, and in organized schools for hundreds of years. Learning also happens in so many parts of our lives: in games, in arts, in community activities, and more.

One useful strategy for the Imagine phase is to focus on coming up with analogies, models, or templates for potential solutions. For instance, in the summer of 2016 I hired the terrific math teacher Michael Pershan to come work in my lab. Michael ran a great blog called Math Mistakes, where he posted interesting examples of incorrect or incomplete student work, and his loyal readers came together to discuss what kind of student thinking might have led students to generate these errors. The conversations were rich and intricate, and I often used the blog in teaching my pre-service students about looking at student work. Our task for the summer was to create a more interactive experience around these kinds of discussions, or, put another way, to make "Math Mistakes: The Game." The goal was to create a kind of "practice space" where my students could engage playfully in carefully looking at student work.

To figure out what this practice space might look like, I brought together a group of math teachers who were on campus at MIT for a summer program and some of my colleagues from the MIT Game Lab. The offices of the Game Lab researchers are covered, wall to wall, with board games. These are people who have played a new game every week or two for years, and their knowledge of games and game mechanics is encyclopedic.

We brought the math teachers and the game experts together in a big conference room filled with materials for game-making—dice, markers, "meeples" (playing pieces that look like people), tokens, Post-Its, posterboard, and so on. Our Discover and Focus work was straightforward—we taught participants the basics of research about looking at student work in mathematics, and we showed them some of the best examples from the Math Mistakes blog.

For the Imagine stage, we worked almost entirely by analogy. Teachers or our game experts would go through games and think about them in the context of Math Mistakes. Taboo with Math Mistakes. Settlers of Catan with Math Mistakes. Gin Rummy with Math Mistakes. Guess Who? with Math Mistakes. With some of these ideas, a small group of participants would be struck by a possibility, and they'd decide to go build a quick prototype. We did this for a couple of hours, and at the end of a session, we played a few early prototypes. They were really fun, and none of them quite worked, but that was fine. We learned to stay away from games that were longer or more complex and focus on mechanics that were built around shorter rounds. All our design successes are built from standing atop large piles of failures, so we were grateful to all of the not-quite-right ideas for helping us reach up to better ones.

A small group of us went to lunch and kept ideating while eating. Eventually, one of my colleagues said, "Math Mistakes with Balderdash," and there was an instant electricity in the room. Balderdash (sometimes called Dictionary) is when you take a real word, one person recites the real definition, three people make up fake definitions, and a judge guesses which is the right one. In about 20 minutes, on a stack of index cards, we made the first version of a game that would be called Baldermath, where four players are given a homework item, and one player is given a piece of incorrect student work and has to make up a rationale for what the student was thinking. The other players then make up incorrect student work and rationales for student thinking, and a judge tries to guess which is the real student mistake. Tricking a judge is fun, guessing correctly is fun, and all the players are naturally engaging in productive practices in looking closely at student work. It took us many tries to figure out that Baldermath had the right mechanic for this practice space, but all of our false starts from many different analogies helped set us up to quickly recognize a powerful idea.[3]

IMAGINING FROM FLARE TO FOCUS

As you get toward the end of the Imagine phase, you will need to shift again from the flare of imagining to the focus of prototyping. Unless you have a big team to work with multiple ideas (like we did during the Math Mistakes workshop), at some point you'll need to select one idea or a cluster of ideas to move into prototyping. As with the Focus phase, where you selected a problem to work on, it's not uncommon for people to get attached to particular potential solutions. When design cycles go through multiple iterations, and there are multiple opportunities for prototyping and testing, it can be easier to say goodbye to ideas that you might come back to.

As someone who manages creative people, one of the main parts of my job is helping people through these transitions. I usually hire or collaborate with people who are more creative, more technically minded, and know specific domains like literacy or computer science better than I do. The folks on my staff are much more likely than I am to come up with brilliant new ideas. A big part of my job in managing teams is helping people recognize where they are in a creative process and where they are going. The most common problem is that people want to linger too long in any given stage, and a big part of my job is to keep teams moving along. Once you've selected a potential solution that could address your "How might we . . ." problem framing, then it's time to get building!

PROTOTYPE

In the previous chapter, I introduced you to Yasmine Kotturi, who taught me a range of techniques and approaches to prototyping. She especially helped me learn that good prototyping is a continuum of activities that move from "low-fidelity" renderings to "high-fidelity" implementations. The word "fidelity" here refers to how closely the prototype matches the final form of whatever you are building. For a new Android app, a low-fidelity prototype might be a few sketches of key software screens drawn onto  index cards. A high-fidelity prototype would be a fully functioning application with a beautifully designed front-end user experience and a working back-end database and software code. For a new unit in a class, a high-fidelity prototype might include a range of slide decks, project worksheets, assessments, readings, and links. A low-fidelity prototype of that unit might be two essential questions, a final project prompt, and a few quick sketches of sample student final work.

There are as many ways to prototype as there are ways to interact with the world, but I like this loose sequence of approaches: sketching and storyboarding, paper prototyping and wireframing, and physical prototyping and rehearsals.

SKETCHING AND STORYBOARDING

Start prototyping by drawing. If you are thinking of a new classroom layout or some other architectural element of school (a hallway mural, new organization of the welcome and administration area to the school, etc.), it's probably obvious that drawing several possible arrangements is a good idea.

In prototyping, I enjoy trying to deliberately find "mismatches" between prototyping forms and the things I'm building. If you are designing a new unit, it's probably obvious to brainstorm lists of essential questions, or key readings, or assessment items. But try this: sketch a moment where a student makes a powerful new connection in your new unit. Draw two mindmaps: one with the set of key schema, ideas, and skills that students are getting from your current instruction, and the second with the schema and skills that students would leave your new unit with. If you are developing new schedules or new community guidelines, it's obvious to brainstorm possible timeblocks for classes or new policies for school grounds, but also draw scenes of what learning will look like when these new administrative policies are in place. I think of these mismatches as "prototyping sideways"; building prototypes in nonobvious forms often gives me new ways of thinking about problems.

When you start drawing, keep it "fat" and go for quantity. Here's Yasmine on using a big pen:

> *One other tip that I like to give is to use a thick pen because it constrains the level of detail that you're able to put into your storyboards and paper prototyping. Often if you use a pencil, it can get too tempting to get into those nitty, gritty details of what exactly your solution idea will look like. So, using that thick pen constrains that level of detail that you're able to add, which then constrains you to thinking at more of a high level.*

To be released from rendering anything with careful or accurate detail is a great gift for people who are terrible at drawing, like me! Also, try to make a lot of drawings quickly. Not only is it another great excuse for having terrible drawings, but then you have lots of opportunities to showcase important directions that your new project might take. In early rounds of prototyping, you might want to make 20 or 30 sketches, and then pick 10 or so to show people in the Try phase, in order to get a sense of where to direct your energy for further prototypes.

One particularly useful form of sketching is storyboarding. As Yasmine describes it, "Storyboarding embodies the narrative aspect of prototyping, where you're showing the story of how someone would be interacting with the idea that you're developing." To start storyboarding, take a regular sheet of paper and fold it in half along the short end. Then, fold the paper into thirds along the long axis. When you unfold the page, you'll have six nice sections like a cartoon panel. Along the top, write some declaration of the distinguishing theme or feature of this prototype, and then draw a story of a community member interacting with your new idea. Show a day in the life of a student in your new classroom, or a teacher's best experience interacting with your new framework for professional learning.

Probably my favorite technique that I learned from Yasmine was to use star people rather than stick people in my storyboarding. To draw a star person, draw a five-point star with one continuous line motion, with a pointy head, two arms out to the sides and two legs pointing down. Add a few quick eyes, a smile or frown or confused face, and put something in the person's hands, a finger to point with, or a little uniform or symbol to distinguish star teachers from star students. Star people have more heft and space in a storyboard than stick people, and they strike most people—drawing them and viewing them—as unusual and unexpected. They pop people into an imaginative space, and they are really fun to draw. That aspect of fun is vital. As Yasmine observes: "I think one thing people often forget about being a designer or engaging in the design thinking process is to just have fun with it. A lot of creativity is sparked when people are relaxed and having a good time, and that's such an important part of a successful design thinking process."

We discuss more about getting feedback in the next section on the Try phase, but the process is simple to start with storyboards.

Make as many as you can; challenge yourself to make 20, and then select 10 different ones to show to people. Get feedback from colleagues, students, and community members about which stories have compelling or repelling elements and use that feedback to work toward sharper ideas in your next round of higher-fidelity prototypes.

PAPER PROTOTYPING AND WIREFRAMING

Sketching and storyboarding are ways of generating impressions, narratives, and key moments from the solution that you are prototyping. Paper prototyping and wireframing are steps toward building more concrete representations of your designs. These two techniques emerge from software design, but they have applications in all kinds of designs.

In the Teaching Systems Lab, when we imagine a new piece of software or app, we often start by building it on paper. For mobile applications, index cards are particularly useful. Turn a 3×5″ card so the short side is on top like a phone. Draw a quick outline of a phone screen and maybe a physical button or interaction menu on the bottom. Then, sketch one key screen for your application. It might have a window with information, some navigation buttons, or other ways of interacting with the application. Imagine that the user presses some important button, and then on another index card, draw the screen that results. Do this for 10 or 20 screens throughout the system. If you want to focus people's attention on certain options, use a highlighter in green or yellow to make them pop out to people.

When you build a paper prototype like this, you can then have people try it out interactively. Sit at a table across from your tester, and hand them the first index card with the first screen. Ask them to interact with it as they would a real phone. When they scroll or click on something, pull out the index card that represents the next screen and lay it on top of the first one. If they move in an unexpected direction, verbally explain the result; if they move in an undesirable direction, steer them toward the choices that you've planned for. Of course, be attentive to what your testers are interested in. If there is a button or choice that a tester is expecting that's not in your prototype, maybe that's the next thing to design!

The first few times you do this, it will feel weird. As Yasmine explains, "It can feel a little silly to go around to all these amazing, intelligent people, and ask them, 'Hey, will you interact with my paper prototype? Will you click on these little fake buttons?' But I think really embracing that discomfort can be great because it is such a powerful technique, and it is often underestimated in how it can be used to communicate ideas." We want prototyping and testing to be light and playful, but it's also okay for some level of discomfort and uncertainty to filter in. Our best ideas often come when we explore new paths, move in new directions, and view problems from new perspectives; leaning into a bit of discomfort is one way to help us see these new vantages.

Of course, you can paper prototype all kinds of things that are not apps. If you are redesigning your classroom layout, get a piece of graph paper and draw the classroom to scale. With another piece of graph paper, cut out shapes to represent desks, tables, chairs, floor rugs, stations, bookcases, and so forth, ideally cutting all of these to scale as well. You can try lots of different layouts without dragging desks around! If you are creating a new unit, course, or curriculum, create a few high-fidelity versions of key elements of that learning experience—a key step in a project sequence, an important set of slides for introducing or reviewing key concepts, a midpoint assessment, discussion questions for a key reading, and so on. Before you flesh out the whole thing, identify some essential elements to get feedback on.

Wireframing is the digital equivalent of paper prototyping, and again it has a history in software design but can have other applications. There are specialized wireframing tools, like Figma or Adobe XD, and they let people without programming expertise create mockups of websites, apps, and digital experiences. You can draw a home screen for an app, create buttons, and have those buttons take users to other screens—like the index cards but digital.

In the Teaching Systems Lab, we often use Google Slides or Microsoft PowerPoint for wireframing and digital prototyping. For instance, some learning management systems allow you to create items or question banks with lots of possible questions that are randomly selected for students in a quiz or assessment. If you want to test new question types, you might write 10 of them up in a set of Google Slides, where it's easy for people to scroll, add comments, and edit, before you input them into your LMS. We have a platform for creating digital clinical simulations for educators called Teacher Moments. Participants are immersed in vignettes of classroom life through audio, video, and text, and then they respond to difficult decisions in teaching through recorded audio and text. People can program these scenarios directly into Teacher Moments, but when we prototype new scenarios, we often write them in Google Slides or Google Docs. Teacher Moments is relatively easy to use, but the familiarity with Google collaboration tools provides a quick path to authoring ideas and getting instant feedback.

PHYSICAL PROTOTYPING AND REHEARSALS

For any kind of tangible product, physical prototyping is an obvious choice. Many teachers use specialized approaches for notebooks, binders, or other mechanisms to help students organize printed materials and take notes. For instance, some curricula encourage the use of "interactive notebooks," where handouts and prepared materials are pasted on the left side of a notebook page, and students take notes or do creative work on the right side of the page. If you are introducing one of these kinds of approaches to students, make one yourself first. Buy the style of notebook you will give away or recommend. Print the kinds of materials that students will file. Practice taking notes as students would in their books. Do a few of the assignments that students will do and file away and start building a physical representation of what your student experience will look and feel like.

Again, in the spirit of sideways prototyping, also consider physically prototyping designs that aren't necessarily physical. If you are planning a new schedule, build a replica of your school building, use coins for students and teachers, and see what it looks like when everyone moves around the building in new ways. Create a replica of the physical setup for a new protocol for a writer's workshop. Have some prepared draft materials and feedback materials at the ready, and let testers jump right into an important moment in the meeting.

Particularly when you are designing anything related to teaching, try to get as quickly as possible to prototyping those actual teaching experiences. I use the term "rehearsal" to refer to an approach to prototyping where designers participate in a live experience of what they are designing. If you are a team of U.S. History teachers building a new unit on Reconstruction, of course lots of your work will be comparing textbooks, winnowing down lists of primary sources, and writing up draft syllabi and assignments in shared documents or spreadsheets. But along with that kind of prototyping, have someone plan 10 or 20 minutes of a lesson on the Compromise of 1877, go to an actual classroom, and teach part of the lesson with colleagues acting as students in a real classroom environment (or, even better, invite real students to participate). In some project-based schools, when teachers practice conducting discrete parts of a project they are called "project slices." A more general term might be "teaching slices," experiences where a design team and community partners immerse themselves in little bits of a new curriculum or teaching approach. It may be difficult to rehearse every possible lesson, workshop, and assignment before rolling out a new curriculum, but it can be quite powerful to participate even in very short bits of mock teaching rehearsal to explore timing, empathize with student experience, and get a sense of what new learning designs feel like during implementation.

TRY

You probably noticed that I already have written quite a bit about playtesting and tryouts in the earlier section on prototyping: showing wireframes to colleagues, doing teaching rehearsals with community members as mock students. It's almost impossible to think or write about prototypes without thinking about the people who will be testing them. But in this section, I share some additional thoughts about when to test, how to test, and who to test with.

WHEN TO TRY OUT YOUR PROTOTYPES

One of the best ways to ensure that you are getting to the Try phase fast enough is to schedule them in advance. Every week in my lab we have a Monday morning stand-up meeting, where we get organized for the week and troubleshoot challenges, and a Friday lab meeting, where we make space to present and give feedback on each other's work. Project teams have weekly meetings, and I meet weekly with most staff. That constellation of meetings means that there is always a time coming up soon, when people working on prototypes can get people together for a tryout.

During periods of intensive development across projects, we also schedule public playtests. A playtest is where we invite anyone connected to education and to our work to come into the lab and kick the tires on whatever we are working on. We typically would set aside one evening a month or every other month and invite people to come to our lab around 5 p.m. We'd play a game or do a brief intro, and then we'd break people up into small groups, typically one group for each of our project teams with something to test. We found that for most activities 40 minutes was a pretty good length of time for a playtest. Of course, there are many learning experiences that take much longer than 40 minutes, but that's enough time for an intro, a teaching slice, feedback, and debrief. When the testing time is constrained, designers need to think carefully about exactly what parts of their design are deserving of feedback.

We usually make time for two of these 40-minute rounds, and then we feed all of our guests dinner and enjoy some conversation and debriefing at the end. By having these regular events become part of the fabric of life in our lab, my students and staff always know that (1) they need to have some significant push forward in their work every 60 days or so, and (2) there would be people ready to test their new designs in that same time frame.

HOW TO TRY OUT YOUR PROTOTYPES

As I mentioned in the previous chapter, every prototype embodies a design hypothesis. A design hypothesis is a designer's belief about the kinds of experiences that participants will have when engaging with a prototype. When we designed the math mistakes game Baldermath, we had a design hypothesis that impersonating students with misconceptions would help teachers adopt more productive approaches to looking at student work. When we designed the Teacher Moments platform for digital clinical simulations, we added a feature where participants could record audio in response to prompts within the simulations. Our design hypothesis was that speaking a response to a situation would provide a more powerful learning experience and better practice experience than simply typing what a person might say.

Write down your design hypothesis! When I'm working with novice designers, I have them fill out a table with four columns. First, what's the feature being tested? Second, what's the design hypothesis of that feature? Third, what would be opposing evidence of that hypothesis—what kinds of evidence might you see in a playtest that would lead you to believe your design hypothesis is wrong? Fourth, what would be confirmatory evidence—the evidence you see or collect if your hypothesis is correct?

When designers spell out these hypotheses and expectations for evidence in advance of a playtest, there are two main benefits. First, you clarify what kinds of evidence you need to be able to collect. Is your hypothesis that a new feature will make participants more engaged? If so, how will you measure that engagement? Will you measure the words they write into a post-activity? A survey measure of satisfaction? The length or intensity of conversation among a group of people? Those are all potentially good measures, but they require different kinds of planning to collect. Second, at every stage of design, it's all too easy to fall in love with our early ideas. Thinking carefully about disconfirmatory evidence—what you would see if your hypothesis is wrong—helps keep you as a designer attentive and open to how your idea might not be working as intended.

Once you have a design hypothesis and plan, the next step is to find people for tryouts and to walk them through the exercise, collecting some data about their experience. Before a tryout, we try to emphasize to playtesters that the way they can help us most is by being very candid with their feedback. We are testing our designs, not them; they can't do anything wrong! The mistakes and problems they experience are our fault. When we playtest things with educators, I'll often make a joke like, "You've probably heard of hamburger feedback where you say something nice for the top bun, then give the meat of the feedback, then say something nice for the bottom bun. Your feedback here can be gluten-free! No buns required; just tell us candidly what you think."

When we are trying out very new prototypes, we are happy to gather people's subjective impressions of a new design: Do they like it? Is it exciting? Does it seem workable? What could be improved? With new designs, we're also more open-ended in our questions about people's experiences, whereas with more refined prototypes, we go into playtests looking for how specific design changes are shaping people's experiences. Meredith Thompson is a user experience researcher who was one of the first members of the Teaching Systems Lab. Here, she talks about doing early-stage playtesting with some of our teaching games:

> *During the more structured playtests, we are often taking notes and making observations as people are playing the game. And then afterwards we'll have a discussion, where we ask different people questions like, "How did that game go for you? What was your experience like? What things worked well? What things maybe would you like to change? And do you have any other feedback for us?" When you're asking testers to give you feedback on a project, it's really good to give them a lot of latitude to basically ask open-ended questions. And that can be very helpful in that you're getting people's experiences; you're not forcing them into*

a box. And so, we often try to make our questions very broad, but are also questions that an individual can answer. Something from their own experience with the game. Not thinking about any of the mechanics, but really the bigger picture, the feel of the game.

However, as our prototypes become more refined, we hold ourselves to increasingly higher standards of evidence, as you can see in the next figure. After early prototypes where we gather subjective impressions and observation notes, we might focus next on artifacts that participants generate in the playtest. If our goal is to help people get better at something (like writing learning objectives for a lesson), can we see evidence that people are thinking about our learning target? Is there evidence of growth or change, even in a short session? After more rounds of design, we might start introducing a "near-transfer task," where we use a pre-post measure to evaluate whether participants are experiencing learning and growth during an activity. When our prototypes are ready for action,

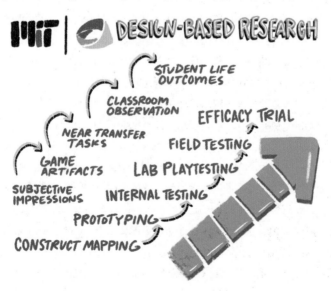

we move them out of lab tests and playtests and into actual schools and classrooms, where we collect increasingly robust data about teacher and student experience and learning.

In the Teaching Systems Lab, most of our design is targeted at improving teacher learning, which is incredibly difficult to measure. Since learning is a change in capacity from one time point to another, you need a baseline measure of proficiency and then at least one additional measure of proficiency during or after a learning activity. It can be quite difficult to collect a baseline measure, do a learning activity, and measure even a tiny change in a 40-minute playtesting window. Nevertheless, we try!

For instance, in our early playtests of Baldermath, we'd start by doing a short Notice and Wonder protocol with participants. They'd look at a typical piece of student work and then identify interesting things to notice and write down their wonderings about student work and thinking. Then we'd play Baldermath and do a similar protocol again at the end. When the game was working, we'd see that participants noticed more and more interesting things with deeper and richer wonderings after playing the game. These kinds of pre and post tasks can be good ways of evaluating design hypotheses specifically related to learning.

It's almost impossible to facilitate a playtest and carefully observe it at the same time, so whenever possible, we assign two people to a playtesting session. One facilitates and the other is responsible for collecting data and observing the session. Sometimes that means doing certain tasks with participants or using a specific observation rubric to confirm or disconfirm some design hypothesis. In the early stages of design, usually we want to take careful observation notes about people's experiences using whatever it is that we've developed.

More than anything else, while playtesting we try to listen and observe people's experiences and bring a sense of humility and skepticism to our work. We put our hearts into our designs, and we badly want them to work brilliantly for the teachers that we serve. So, we need to balance that with the humility and skepticism that our ideas often have shortcomings or just plain don't work, and we serve our communities better when we maintain vigilance about our flaws and are iterating to improve them.

WHO SHOULD TRY OUT YOUR PROTOTYPES

One of the major disadvantages of doing learning design at MIT is that people who find themselves at MIT are for the most part not teachers and not typical learners. In the Teaching Systems Lab, we primarily design learning experiences for K–12 teachers and pre-service teachers. There are no practicing K–12 teachers at MIT. We have lots of recent high school students, but weird ones who really loved school and excelled at most of what they tried to do there.

If you do design work in a district office, you might face a similar problem, where much of your design is focused on students, teachers, or parents at the margins of the system, but everyone surrounding you is deeply invested and experienced in the core of schools. Of course, that expertise has all kinds of advantages, but when you try out prototypes with people who are very different from the intended users, you can get feedback that leads you in the wrong direction. For those of you doing design work with the people you are trying to serve every day, you have a huge advantage! Use that closeness to try out prototypes with authentic users early and often.

Whenever possible, you should try out learning designs with the community members who are going to be the beneficiaries of a new design. If you are designing new assessments, curricula, teaching techniques, or schedules, try them out with the students and teachers who will actually be engaged in these activities. If you are designing new resources and approaches for parent engagement, it's better to try those kinds of things out with parents and family members who are on the margins, rather than those who are deeply engaged.

That said, it's often difficult to have enough testing opportunities with the best possible people for tryouts. At MIT, we have nearly limitless resources for doing tryouts with our own staff, all of whom have been students and many of whom have been teachers. For classroom teachers, at first it may feel easier to try out new designs with fellow teachers rather than students. That's fine. Do early-stage tryouts with any convenient sample of people willing to test something new. As your prototypes become more refined and high fidelity, you can invest more resources in gathering the best possible playtesters for your new designs.

In good design, when you find yourself on the right track, you'll experience lots of iterative microcycles of refining prototypes and collecting new evidence from tryouts. These cycles have a spiral progression. You'll start with low-fidelity prototypes, and over time the prototypes will become increasingly high fidelity. You might start tryouts looking for open-ended subjective evidence: Do kids like this activity? Is this approach working for teachers? As your prototype gets refined, you might start looking for more objective measures of efficacy: Are students learning more or are teachers implementing new techniques? Throughout this process, you might start your early tryouts with anyone nearby you can find like close friends, colleagues, or students. However, as you get closer to a final design, you will want to ensure that your tryouts engage the community members who will benefit from your designs.

Eventually, prototyping and tryouts will morph naturally into implementation. Your prototype will become the thing you do, and your tryouts will be your everyday practice. If successful, this great innovation will become another common practice, woven into the routine of your work in schools and classrooms. As the new practice settles in, your design eye will turn to new frontiers where there is space for improvement.

REFLECT AND SHARE

DESIGN CRITS

Academic programs for art, architecture, and design have well-established protocols for sharing work, soliciting feedback, and reflecting on the process and product: the design critique session, sometimes just called a "crit." Design crits are markers of completion, moments of celebration, and opportunities for learning.

Many educators have facilitated these kinds of sessions: art teachers do public displays, STEM teachers facilitate science fairs, language teachers host public readings, and so forth. In Chapter 2, on the Cycle of Experiment and Peer Learning, I described the "teaching fair" at the Peel School Board where educators shared their teaching innovations. As with many of the steps in Design Thinking for Leading and Learning, educators bring valuable teaching experience that they can draw upon in their own design work.

A good design crit has several key components. First, the experience is public and brings in a range of people to help offer feedback. In most school contexts, it's valuable to invite the "clients" of a design exercise, like students, teachers, and community members, to an event. It is also useful to invite domain experts. A design fair on STEM teaching would benefit from bringing in other STEM department heads, experts in STEM research from local colleges and universities, or employers who hire and train STEM graduates. Diverse perspectives can help you evaluate your work from new dimensions.

Second, design crits publicly display prototypes, implementations, and evidence from tryouts. Ideally, host the event in a space that's big enough to let people move through physical prototypes, act out rehearsals, and play with digital prototypes on big screens where groups of people can watch the activity together. Great design crits feel like museums, where participants are immersed in exhibits from design.

Good design crits invite public reflection. In a small group, you might invite each design team member to prepare a small presentation on their experience and learning. In bigger groups, you might organize the event around "stations" like the Peel teaching fair, or you might have participants write up short reflections, like the short annotations that accompany art displayed at a museum. A major part of preparing for a public critique event should be allowing design team members to reflect on their experience and learning.

Finally, design crits should solicit feedback. Provide participants with a chance to make public remarks, or respond to design examples with surveys, rubrics, or other feedback mechanisms.

If you can do these kinds of exercises in the middle of a design cycle, then the feedback and criticism can be used to refine the direction of prototypes and testing. Oftentimes, though, these events are hosted at the end of a design cycle, where it might be that unworkable ideas are shelved or good ideas shift toward steady implementation rather than rapid cycles of ongoing refinement. Both things are normal! All good design sits atop a pile of unsuccessful efforts and we don't have time in schools to tinker with everything forever.

When your reflection and sharing come at the end of a design cycle, it can be more important to reflect on process than product, especially if the product will be fixed and steady for a while. What did you learn about working together as a design team? What design processes accelerated your learning and work, and where did you feel most stuck? What will you do differently in your next design cycle to make things work better? What will you do in your next design cycle to include more voices, and elevate perspectives of those in your community who should be heard more?

CONCLUSION

As I said at the outset, design is a set of practices, not a single script or recipe. Your approach to design will depend on the strengths and limitations of your team members, the amount of time and resources available, your context, problem of practice, and many other factors. As you incorporate iterative design in your work, you will develop more tools and protocols in your set of practices, and you will come to understand what works with your team and context.

In my years of leading organizations that are committed to improvement through design, I've found it's important to balance a set of traditions with a sense of novelty. Part of what defines the Teaching Systems Lab as an organization is the practices that we have adopted and maintained over many years. Every project starts with a "Mother Doc"—a collaborative online document that includes a running record of meeting notes, links to other key documents, and ultimately an archive of all the key moments in a project. Creating a new Mother Doc becomes an exciting moment in the lab, a marker of when something new is beginning to take shape. You really can't do a project in my lab without one.

While that practice is fixed in our lab, I am also conscious that our design team is made from a constantly rotating cast of characters. New students join the lab; postdocs get faculty jobs and new postdocs take on their roles; and we bring in new collaborators for different projects. For them to feel a sense of ownership, it's important that part of our design practices and collaborative routines change with each year and each project, and that team members have some input in those changes. When we work together on a new design effort, our work should feel like we're building on a solid tradition of well-established practice that makes us feel like we are part of an established community. At the same time, our collaborative work should feel fresh and new, particular to the specific people who are working together and the specific problem that we are tackling. (Amusingly enough, several days after writing this paragraph, one of my teams decided they wanted to adopt a new project management software for their project. I hate it! I don't want to learn a new thing! But it doesn't matter, because they like it, and part of my job is giving the ownership of the design process to them.)

As you start new design processes in your environment, you might think about what routines are special to your organization that you want to draw upon as you begin a new initiative, and what new practices you should invent together to make each design cycle feel fresh and to make sure that each design team feels ownership and investment in your work.

My final advice is this: there is no other way to learn Design Thinking for Leading and Learning except to dive in and do it. So, find a few colleagues, hop over to the design walkthroughs that are available online (wiley.com/go/iterate), and commit to spending a few days or weeks taking on one of the two design challenges offered.

THE COLLABORATIVE INNOVATION CYCLE

WHAT IS THE COLLABORATIVE INNOVATION CYCLE?

One of the most inspiring public schools to visit is High Tech High in San Diego. It's a project-based learning school, powerfully captured in the documentary film *Most Likely to Succeed*. The best way to see the school is on a tour with the school's founder, Larry Rosenstock. The building is a kind of giant warehouse, with classrooms enclosed by glass and open meeting spaces in between. Larry can point to almost any element of the school and

describe the purpose behind it. The glass walls promote transparency and public display; the classrooms are connected into teacher office spaces that promote collaboration; the high ceilings allow for public display of (large) student projects; the open meeting spaces transform easily into small presentation spaces for end-of-term student presentations on their work. Every college counselor in the school is themselves a first-generation college student with several years of experience working in college admissions. There is a profound sense of coherence to the school. You can talk with teachers, students, parents, and school leaders, and they will tell you the same story about the schools' values and priorities. You can walk around the building and see those values brought to life in design.

Design is about balancing tensions, and coherence and experimentation can often be at odds. Experimentation is when a part of the whole diverges from the well-worn path to discover something new; coherence is when the whole moves in concert. In the previous two cycles we focused more on the experiment side of the ledger; in this chapter, we discuss generating and managing coherence.

In gym class as a child, my favorite days were when the teacher brought out the giant parachute for us to play with. We'd stand in a big circle holding the edge of the fabric. On the first count of three we'd lift our arms in the air and the parachute would loft up. Then, on a second count of three, we'd rotate our arms behind us so a little patch of fabric went underneath our tuckus, and we'd sit down with the edge of the parachute beneath us and the dome of the chute all around us. And then, oh the games you could play! We'd take turns being the tent pole in the middle, or we'd play Cat and Mouse, with the mice scurrying under the chute and the Cat trying to tag them from on top. You could sneak in and out of the chute, you could rest underneath it, and you could marvel at it from the outside. But all of these roles—cat and mouse and tentpole—depended on everyone deciding to play parachute together.

Using the Cycle of Experiment and Peer Learning, we investigated how change permeates through schools, from small classroom experiments, through the reflection of teaching teams, and onward through sharing across faculty. Since schools are fine-grained, loosely-coupled institutions, this work of experimentation is inherently and intensely local. Teachers are energized by autonomy, and they are motivated by the specific challenges of their classrooms and contexts.

If all experimentation is local, individual, and idiosyncratic, then individual teachers can improve, but schools as systems and communities don't get any better. It is entirely possible for a math teacher to make substantial improvements behind closed doors, and then leave or retire without their grade-level team or department colleagues benefiting at all from that improvement. For schools to improve as systems, there need to be structures and leadership that help create shared instructional language, vision, and purpose. Like the gym class parachute, that sense of common purpose needs to be capacious enough that teachers from different grades and specialties can find their own individual place within that common purpose but constrained enough that teachers from different specialties feel some measure of common cause.

Leadership in schools is about balancing these tensions. Schools need to simultaneously allow individual teacher expression and experimentation while encouraging those individual efforts to be part of a common cause.

In this chapter and the next, I introduce the Collaborative Innovation Cycle, a design cycle that explores how school leaders can foster a sense of coherence while leading change. If the core of Design Thinking for Leading and Learning is about conducting meaningful experiments, then the heart of the Collaborative Innovation Cycle is about creating collaborative environments in which experimentation, experience, and reflection are part of a common cause. The work we do together in these chapters involves seeing schools as systems and aligning the different parts and diverse stakeholders in a complex system.

FOUR PHASES OF THE COLLABORATIVE INNOVATION CYCLE

As in the previous approaches to iterative design, I represent the Collaborative Innovation Cycle with a starting point and a series of phases, but this simplifies a messy process where teams and communities are often moving through multiple phases at the same time. The Collaborative Innovation Cycle has four phases: Bringing People Together Around Ideas They Care About; Refining a Vision and Getting to Work; Working Together Through Ups and Downs; and Measuring Progress and Adjusting. In this chapter, I've ordered the phases beginning with Bringing People Together Around Ideas They Care About, but your school can start anywhere on this cycle. In fact, many schools may choose to start with Measuring Progress and Adjusting, taking stock of what has and hasn't worked with initiatives they've recently tried.

The first part of the Collaborative Innovation Cycle is deliberately subversive. Usually, we think of leadership as a process in which leaders tell followers where to go or what to do. Here, I'll ask you to start your leadership work by asking where the people in your community want to go. Your school has a history and a culture, filled with strengths, successes, and opportunities. Leadership starts with understanding, honoring, and respecting what people have already accomplished, and then helping them come together around ideas that will take their work forward. The futurist William Gibson said that "The future is already here, it just isn't evenly distributed."[1] Your first job as a leader is to sense and pay attention to what people are doing that already is important and can be built upon.

Even if leaders, school principals, or superintendents don't unilaterally set a direction, they do shine a light. The second phase of the Launching Innovation cycle is Refining a Vision and Getting to Work. Our goal in this phase is to try to bring people's diverse ideas and perspectives together around a shared vision. The signature quality of our very best schools is coherence. As I mentioned earlier with High Tech High, when you walk through the halls of a great school with its principal, they can point out to you how everything hangs together, how the core values of the schools are expressed in school routines and teacher practices, in student work. That happens over time as people come together around ideas they care about and focus on something together that's worth improving.

As I've emphasized in Design Thinking for Leading and Learning, a crucial part of innovation is just getting started. Our model of leadership is not heavy on figuring everything out in advance and developing elaborate plans but, rather, embracing a bias to action. There's a genius in the simple act of tackling challenges even when you don't have every possible step plotted out. There is no recipe that I can share, or that you can follow, for leading your school to excellence. Rather, you will learn what works and what doesn't as you are engaging in change activities and getting others to help you in reflecting on how it's working.

As this work goes forward, you will inevitably move into the third phase of the cycle, Working Together Through Ups and Downs. Launching and nurturing innovation is exciting. If it wasn't, you wouldn't do it. But it's also challenging, emotionally difficult work. Collaborative work is fraught with all the challenges of working together: loss, resistance, and conflict. Working with people is also full of encouragement, shared joy, combined efforts, and celebration, but the downsides are part of a package with these benefits. These are normal, natural, inescapable parts of working toward change. My MIT colleague Peter Senge often tells groups of leaders that it is a mistake to think of leadership as "neck up" work, all head and no heart. Addressing emotions is an inevitable part of managing change and working with people through conflict is a central part of the Collaborative Innovation Cycle.

We will explore how communication, especially listening, is at the heart of collaboration, and we'll examine specific strategies for making listening, communication, and collaboration more effective. These strategies won't let you avoid hard times and hard conversations, but they offer new tools to manage those challenges and lead others through them.

Finally, if anything is worth doing, it's worth measuring whether or not it's working. A crucial part of launching change is Measuring Progress and Adjusting. Part of this work is technical, evaluating whether new instructional practices are leading to better learning. And a huge part of this work is cultural, creating the conditions where teachers and administrators can look at evidence, share their candid perspectives, and figure out together how to continually improve. The schools that can figure out this step of constant experimentation, evaluation, and adjustment become learning organizations, places where every student, teacher, and administrator in a building can constantly learn and grow.

FOUR LEVELS OF CHANGE

In developing the ideas of the Collaborative Innovation Cycle, I had the good fortune to work with Peter Senge from the MIT Sloan School of Management. Together, we co-taught Launching Innovation in Schools, and all of the online courseware from that work is available at the MIT Open Learning Library and licensed for sharing and reuse. (You can access the materials at openlearninglibrary.mit.edu and search for "Launching Innovation in Schools" or directly at https://openlearninglibrary.mit.edu/courses/course-v1:MITx+11.154x+3T2018/about.) In the 1990s, Peter wrote one of the most widely read leadership texts of the twentieth century, *The Fifth Discipline*.[2] In this book, Peter argues for business firms to think of themselves as learning organizations. In learning organizations, as people do the work of the firm—buying, making, selling, trading—they are also constantly engaged in learning and improving. For schools to become learning organizations, it's not enough to have just young people learning. Everyone in the school community should be learning and growing as they engage with their day-to-day work. For that learning to happen, leaders need to see their organizations as complex systems, crafted from all the personal relationships that exist within the organization and all the connections pointing from the organization outward into the wider world.

One of Peter's most useful insights about change is that it has to operate at four different levels: self, team, organization, and community. The middle two levels of systems are obvious sites for improvement. In schools, much of the action is in small groups and teams, like a teacher's classroom or a team of collaborating teachers. These teams operate in an organization—for most people, a single school building. That school is situated in a broader community—a city, a county, a province or state, a country—and that broader community has norms, values, policies, expectations, political conflicts, and history. And the final of these four levels is the self—our own identity and actions.

When I helped run a summer camp in my carefree youth, one of our training exercises was to roleplay a student who was stubbornly refusing to talk. One of the takeaways from the exercise was that we who ran the camp—counselors, staff, directors—were absolutely powerless to make a child speak if he or she didn't want to. The people around us have incredible autonomy and agency. The only thing that we can truly control is ourselves: the assumptions, energy, and openness that we bring to a difficult situation, the way we choose to listen, and what we choose to say and do. Sometimes leaders shy away from these dimensions of leadership, but take it from a couple of faculty at clinical, quantitative MIT: there is no way to escape the role of emotions and self-reflection in leadership. For many of the most important efforts in the Collaborative Innovation Cycle, leading change starts with thinking about how we will change ourselves.

With a view that leadership is something that we do with others and we do inside ourselves, let's dig into the parts of our last framework, the Collaborative Innovation Cycle!

BRINGING PEOPLE TOGETHER AROUND IDEAS THEY CARE ABOUT

Whenever I launched a consulting engagement with a new school or district, I would start by asking them about their recent history. What kinds of things are you and your colleagues already excited about? What are the goals that you have for your students that seem most urgent and most dear? What are the recent initiatives that your colleagues look back on as successes? What have you been working on in the past few months?

Someone in the school or district invited me because they thought that doing more with technology would help make the school a better place. But that position was rarely widely held among all the faculty. There are lots of things that could make schools better; maybe technology was one of them and maybe learning to teach with new technology was just a lot of additional work.

Every community has a history, a culture, and a set of values. They have past experiences with professional learning and improvement. They have a sense of their strengths and shortcomings. They have ideas about improving teaching and learning that they care deeply about. Those highly-valued ideas are the catalyst for unlocking their time, energy, and commitment. When I worked with schools on technology consulting, I wasn't trying to get them to adopt an approach to technology instruction that I was bringing with me.

Instead, I was trying to figure out what they cared most about, and then work with them to think about how technology could help them achieve those precious goals.

This process is, inevitably, a dance back and forth between leadership and community. If things are going according to plan, leadership has expertise. Leadership knows stuff. Leadership has a wider view of the whole landscape and the complex system of school. Assigning people into leadership roles is good; we need someone to take the job of pointing communities in the direction of change.

All of that expertise and authority must be balanced by the realization that the work of schools is granular and that school staff can exercise tremendous autonomy. Teachers have a well-documented capacity to ignore school leadership, either through outright refusal or through a well-honed art of minimal compliance. You can force teachers to write lesson objectives on the board, and they might dutifully write them up there every morning and then go on teaching, with them and their students devoting not a single brain cell to those objectives for the rest of the day. Most change initiatives depend on the goodwill of educators buying into new ideas, spending discretionary time (both paid and unpaid), and carrying out an initiative.

Getting a school community engaged in the work of change starts with listening to them. In Chapter 1, we heard a lot from Kate Lewis, a teacher in central Massachusetts, about her experience with experimenting in her teaching. Let's return to the same school district, and read thoughts from her colleagues, then-assistant superintendent Mary Beth Banios and director of instructional technology Shawna Powers, about how to make listening a systemic part of leadership practice and a school community.

Mary Beth Banios (speaking as assistant superintendent for curriculum, instruction, and assessment for the Shrewsbury Public Schools): *We are a very collaborative district. We have faculty advisory councils, where myself and our superintendent and our HR director gather with teacher representatives from every school once a month to hear what's working, what's not working, what are some of the issues that you're hearing about that we need to be paying attention to. I think being collaborative means really honoring multiple perspectives. And I think that Shrewsbury really—works really hard to get a lot of voices in any initiative—voices of teachers, voices of administrators, voices of students, voices of community members, and in the case of our innovation and learning study group, the school committee members as well. And I think that that way of doing business or making decisions trickles down.*

Shawna Powers: *So then when you are a department director, let's say, and then you're making decisions within your department, you employ a similar methodology in terms of how you go about making decisions. And then I think that trickles out into the classroom, where if people are accustomed to working in environments where their input is sought, they're more likely to seek input from their students. So, I really think it's really about empowering each and every individual learner, whether the learner is an adult learner or a student learner.*

Here, Mary Beth and Shawna illustrate how personal leadership and personal change are intimately connected with systems change. As district leaders, Mary Beth and Shawna believe that listening to the community is a vital part of their work, and they organize their schedules and work practices to ensure that they have adequate time and space for listening. As they role-model active listening and community engagement as leaders, that spreads throughout the district and down into the schools, and faculty start embracing the idea that listening is an important part of leadership and teaching.

FOUR QUESTIONS FOR INNOVATION

The place to start collaborative innovation is not with what leadership thinks should happen (or not just what leadership thinks should happen), but with what people in classrooms and working close with children think is important. In the next chapter, I'll walk you through one of my favorite activities to do with school communities that I call Four Questions for Innovation. I've done this activity with entire faculty teams in big gymnasiums and with small district leadership teams in conference rooms. The heart of the activity is asking people four questions:

1. What are the signature strengths of your school?
2. What are the most important learning goals that you have for your students?
3. What are the major initiatives going on right now?
4. What are the most promising areas where new innovations could improve learning in your school?

Folks write responses to these questions on sticky notes, and they post them on big walls, usually situated in the four corners of a room. Then we organize the stickies into themes, and for each of the four questions for innovation, I encourage different kinds of reflection.

When people list signature strengths, those are the resources that our change initiative—whatever it ends up being—is going to draw on. Whenever people talk about signature strengths related to professional learning, my ears always perk up, because that points a light to where the improvement pathways will be. Some schools have incredible experiences with professional learning communities

(PLCs), and teachers will tell you that the best improvement work happens there. PLCs it is then! And at other schools, they will tell you that the PLCs are a disaster and a complete waste of time. In those schools, we need to develop some new pathway for teacher collaborative learning to happen. Nothing in education simply works; everything works for some communities, at some times, for some topics or circumstances, and not others.

When people express their most important learning goals for students, they are describing their most closely held professional values. Those values are key sources of motivation for people, and they are slow to change. Any improvement pathway is going to be much easier if plans embrace those values, rather than moving around them or against them.

In technology leadership consulting, one of my main tasks was convincing leadership that technology wasn't really their end goal. The best way to frame any technology initiative is around the goals that a community already embraces. If a high school really cares about preparing students for college and career, then the job of a technology initiative is to make the school better at that preparation. If an elementary school is concerned about reading readiness, then any technology initiative has to account for how it will advance that important goal.

Asking faculty about their current and ongoing initiatives provides a crucial barometer of a school system's capacity for additional change. Sometimes, I would visit a school or district, and 20 or 30 participants would write up three sticky notes about what the school was working on, and a small number of key themes and initiatives would become immediately apparent. If everyone in a school system says they are working on the same few things, then that is a school with coherent improvement plans and probably organized leadership and a sense of community and collaboration among faculty. Schools where everyone is working together on a few things are usually schools that know how to get things done to get better.

But sometimes I'd visit a school, and their improvement efforts would be highly individualized or all over the place. Sometimes they would be coherent—in that every initiative had at least a few people who devoted a sticky note to highlighting the work—but just overwhelmingly numerous.

Schools, in the best of circumstances, are incredibly busy and complex places. Most schools can only effectively manage a few improvement initiatives at any given time. That's not necessarily a criticism—school improvement is hard—but a recognition of the reality that schools are more likely to make improvements when they can identify a small number of areas for improvement, work on them, make progress, stabilize those improvements, and then find other things to work on.

Using this barometer of "initiative density" and "initiative fatigue," I would sometimes coach school leaders into finding ways to be more targeted and coherent in their approach to change. When schools had too many initiatives underway, I would ask them to consider which of these efforts most connected to their key learning goals for students. Which built on their signature strengths? When people are working on things that address their strengths and most closely held values, they are more likely to feel motivated, confident, and persistent.

My final question for these groups was about innovation and the future. I would ask faculty and leaders, "What are the best possible uses for technology in teaching and learning?" or more generally, "What are the innovations that are most likely to improve teaching and learning?"

Of the four questions, this one points toward new areas and efforts where schools might have weaknesses or shortcomings. And of course, schools need to do new things, and they need to stretch and grow in areas where they might have a lack of experience or atrophied muscles. But the key insight of the entire Four Questions for Innovation exercise is that any new initiative in a school depends immensely on the other three topics that we discussed together: what a community takes pride in, what they value, and what they are already doing. In technology consulting, this meant encouraging schools to avoid, whenever possible, generating a brand-new "technology initiative." Nobody wants new batteries to charge, new software to learn, or expensive new devices to care for. But educators very, very much want their students to learn more and to be better prepared, and they want to work with their colleagues on improvement efforts that will lead to better learning. In many cases, therefore, the best way to frame a new initiative is not as a break with the past, but as a continuation of values and of prior good work—as the extension of an existing initiative rather than a brand-new direction or, worse, "one more thing to do."

The Four Questions for Innovation activity is one efficient and enjoyable way to surface the issues the people care most about and then bring people together around those issues. When leaders can see what schools are doing and where they are headed, they can chart a way forward that respects and honors the core values and expertise of the faculty community.

REFINING A VISION AND GETTING TO WORK

If people are going to work together, they need something to work together toward: a shared vision. In the Four Questions for Innovation activity, the writing and brainstorming starts with individual contributions. Each person gets to write their own individual responses to how they see their signature strengths and how they view their most important learning goals. Then people take their individual ideas and put them on walls as sticky notes. Next, people start moving the notes around, finding common themes, and looking for points of connection or tension. The individual aspects of personal vision start to cohere into themes that can be the source of a shared vision.

One of the places near me where you can see the personal visions of educators come together into a shared vision for a whole school is the Benjamin Banneker Charter School in Cambridge, Massachusetts, which enrolls students from all over the Boston area. Banneker defines themselves as an elementary STEM school. That doesn't mean that they call their science classes "STEM" and then just go about doing whatever they were doing before. It means they ask themselves iteratively and constantly, "How do we integrate STEM into our daily practices and how do we create pathways for our young students to find their way into the incredible STEM opportunities in the Boston area?" My team spoke to two Banneker educators—teacher Meredith Daley and principal Sherley Bretous—and in the following case study, they describe what it means for a whole community to be devoted to an educational ideal.

> SHERLEY BRETOUS (principal): *For us, part of the problem was our kids weren't seeing themselves reflected in the science and technology fields. Our girls weren't seeing themselves reflected, and our African American students, and our Brown children, our children of color. We're in Cambridge, Mass. So, when we started asking local communities and community colleges and other*

(Continued)

*institutions around here for something as simple as having a pro-
fessional night, we would want a Black professor or a Black sci-
entist or a woman, it's not as easy as it sounded. So, we thought,
okay, if we can get our kids in love with science and use the technology to enhance their learning experience, we've got it. So,
when I think of Banneker as a STEM school, we think, okay, what
does that mean? What does it look like in elementary school?*

MEREDITH DALEY (teacher): *As a STEM school, we try to
integrate STEM throughout our day. Students know that it's our
main focus and main vision here at the Banneker. And right now,
we're working on a living things unit. And we've planted bean
seeds. So, they can observe those bean seeds and watch those
bean seeds grow. So, throughout the day students are integrating that into each subject area that we're doing. In reading
they're reading about a plant's life and how plants grow. They've
experimented with different ways that those bean seeds could
grow. They've done some math around it. They are taking data
and measurements. They're collecting different ideas about
what that bean seed might become, what they could do with it
once it's fully grown. So, our whole day that bean seed, this little
tiny bean seed, is integrated into each part of our day.*

SHERLEY BRETOUS: *When we became a STEM school, it
was an arduous process. We spent a great deal of time thinking
about: What does that look like? What is it we want for our students? We met with the board members. We met with families.
We met with students. We interviewed students and parents.
We interviewed local community members and local businesses.
And we went to each table with the big questions, like does this
mean an extended day for us? Then we talked about what's positive, what might work, what might not work, what are some
of the obstacles. So, we spent a lot of time thinking about our
school day, the amount of work that our students were expected
to do, then we wanted to know, what does success look like?
After year one? After year two? How will it impact our day to*

day? How will it impact our state assessments? Because as a charter school, we are mandated to meet certain standards. And whenever you're learning something new, there's a dip. And how will that work for us? How will we be able to explain it? How will we look at the data? What data can we expect? It was all tenuous. And it was all new. But it was exciting.

When you're trying to get everyone on the same page, when you're trying to build a culture of collaboration, a shared vision, there are several different pitfalls that can happen. One is that lack of clarity. Ensuring that everyone understands what the end goal is. And sometimes you don't know. But I think you have to keep delving deeper and deeper and deeper, until you clarify what you want that vision to be. And then I think we spent a great deal around process. Because as a team, you now know the vision. We have to figure out, well, how do we share that out? How do we make sure everyone's on the same page and that it's not top down? It's me telling you what my vision is, but that you feel invested in it, and that you feel heard about it.

THE SOMEDAY/MONDAY DILEMMA

It's exciting to read from Meredith and Sherley about how they developed, nurtured, and maintained a shared vision of STEM education for Banneker. The best efforts at creating a shared vision for a school's future balance being ambitious and achievable; I call that the Someday/Monday dilemma.

The Banneker educators explain how full-day integrated STEM instruction was a real stretch for their whole faculty and leadership community. Implementing it required personal growth, changes in the classroom and the whole school institution, and then new kinds of engagement with the community. It required change on all four levels: personal, team, organization, and community contexts.

When you have those ambitious goals of what teaching could look like Someday, then you have a vision to work toward. But you will not be able to implement that vision tomorrow—it's too big and too hard and there is too much to learn. So, the challenge is to find something that you can do on Monday that you are able to implement. What is one step that you can take toward your powerful learning environment? What is the MVP—the minimum viable product—of your Someday vision? What's one part of that you can put into practice right away?

Big changes in schools, like implementing major pedagogical improvements, require shifting multiple parts of the school experience. They require new curriculum, new schedules, new teacher training, new student and family expectations, new resources, and more. It's typically impossible for any organization to change all those things at once. It's daunting and difficult to muster all the needed resources at the same time. Usually, you can't convince all the necessary stakeholders of the urgency of change all at once.

I think of all these changes as levers, and a big pedagogical change requires pulling eight or nine levers at once, which is impossible in most school contexts. So, you pull one or two. The beauty of pulling one or two is that it's achievable. You can do it with a big group of educators, or you can do it with a small group of pilot teachers. You prove that something new can work. You refine those two levers, and you understand better what needs to change with the other seven. You have some evidence and some political capital to bring your colleagues and community about making more changes. The way you get to the great big new Someday across the giant river of change is by laying down Monday stones one at a time in front of you.

Now, I don't mean to say that the road between Monday and Someday is easy traveling. When you need to change nine things, and you only change two, things don't exactly work. There are many schools that have embraced project-based learning approaches by starting with new curriculum and lessons. But, if your periods are 42 minutes long, it doesn't matter what curriculum you use, you won't have enough time for project work. At the same time, you probably will never convince your colleagues and school board that you should rearrange the schedule to get 84 minutes with your students if you can't demonstrate some good progress—a good MVP—with 42 minutes.

It's also entirely possible that as you make one little Monday change at a time, the rest of the system reacts with conservative impulses. You push forward in one direction, and the system pushes back, and all the little Mondays don't lead to a big brand-new Someday.

But for all those challenges, it's very rarely the case in education that the best, most practical way forward is with one giant untested wholesale shift. Typically, the best approach is to collectively develop an ambitious shared vision, woven together from many different personal visions. Then, people get to work in their individual contexts or in small teams, starting with Monday-sized initiatives to bring new ideas to life. Once your shared vision has started to take shape, once you have some Monday-sized ideas with which to get started, then it's time to embrace a bias to action and get to work!

GETTING TO WORK: THE CYCLE OF EXPERIMENT AND PEER LEARNING, AND DESIGN THINKING FOR LEADING AND LEARNING

Once you have begun cobbling together a provisional shared vision, it's time to get to work. And if you have made it this far in this book, then you know a lot about getting specific change initiatives started! It starts with frontline educators conducting new experiments, and all the tips, tricks, and guides from Design Thinking for Leading and Learning are going to be valuable tools in your belt. These tools will be even more powerful when you are conducting experiments not just as a lone wolf educator, but as part of a team of colleagues with an emerging shared vision, looking to collaboratively make important improvements in your school. Lots of that work is still local, but ideally you and your colleagues will find points of intersection that spur and support your individual interventions.

If you are a school leader ministering to faculty who are getting to work on experimentation, then the Cycle of Experiment and Peer Learning can be a powerful set of tools for guiding your leadership practice. You understand that your job is to keep these cycles of design, experimenting, planning, and reflection spinning efficiently and joyfully. You can provide resources for additional experimentation, support the work of team-based reflection, and generate opportunities for the peer-to-peer learning that is the essential ingredient for teachers to change their practice. With your emerging shared vision, and the work of adopting a shared instructional language, you can help ensure that the individual, local experiments happening across your classrooms and learning spaces add up together to systemic change.

One final reminder and benediction here about getting to work: you don't start the work of change after you have figured out what it is you want to do and you've gotten everyone on board. *Starting the work is how you get people on board. Starting the work is how you figure out what it is that you want to do.* The Collaborative Innovation Cycle is about building these broader cycles of collaboration and community wayfinding into the design process. You bring people together around ideas they care about, and you refine a vision, and you guide people toward a place where they are clear enough to take some Monday-sized steps toward your goal. People individually and in teams then get to work, conducting design experiments, exploring what the shared problem looks like in their individual contexts, testing hypotheses about what works and what doesn't, and refining new ideas and practices through cycles of exploration, design, testing, and reflection. Those design experiments will reveal new insights about what works, what's important, and how best to understand the nature of obstacles and challenges. Those insights feed back into bringing people together around ideas they care about, and then refining future visions and launching new work.

This work can be fun and exciting, but it also inevitably creates friction and conflict.

WORKING TOGETHER THROUGH UPS AND DOWNS

As I've noted since the first chapter, on the Cycle of Experiment and Peer Learning, change is inherently bound up with loss.

When new designs are implemented, people often feel the loss of the familiar immediately, and they come to recognize the benefits of change slowly. Teaching requires deep personal investment, so conversations and plans for change can easily become heated. We build school buildings in ways that wall adults off from one another, and without travel and effort we literally cannot see what the work of school looks like from other people's point of view easily. These are all potential sources of conflict. They can all be overcome, and innovation and improvement can be joyful work, but we need to be honest with ourselves and our colleagues that friction and conflict are normal.

This domain—Working Together Through Ups and Downs—is where I personally have learned the most over the past decade. When Peter Senge and I were developing an online course called *Launching Innovation in Schools*, he proposed adding a unit about collaboration and communication. I thought to myself, "No, Peter, that's material for a different course. This is a course about getting things done and making change, not smoothing over people's feelings." But as we talked more and I learned more, I came to understand how Peter was right and how my blind spot was a common one.

Recall that Peter Senge teaches at the MIT Sloan School of Management. As you might imagine, MIT is not necessarily the most touchy-feely of places. Much of the work throughout the university— "The Institute," as we call it—is quite quantitative and empirical. It is a place where many people are comfortable with numbers and data, and more than a few of my students and colleagues do not specialize in being in touch with their feelings.

Peter and his colleagues in Management have spent decades on a research journey in their careers trying to understand the conditions under which firms—banks, factories, retailers, schools, universities, nonprofits—are successful. People come together in firms to accomplish what they could not accomplish alone, so it makes sense that teams are the vital unit of progress and accomplishment in an organization. Teams are where the work of change and improvement gets done.

What, then, accounts for successful teams? It turns out that a key component of successful teams is their communication. Effective communication is not the absence of conflict; divergent ideas and perspectives are essential to good design. Effective communication allows for conflict and manages those tensions and even outbreaks. When teams can communicate toward common aims, air disagreements, and resolve some of those disagreements while tolerating those that remain, then those groups of people have the potential to get a lot of great work done. Indeed, Peter explains that one way to define teams is as groups of people who participate in conversations:

> *If we're really serious about collaborating, then we're really serious about the subject of conversation. Collaboration has very little meaning if we're not starting to pay a different quality of attention to what's happening in our conversations. Conversation is inescapable. You might say conversation is the core process in any organization, in any work setting. But we actually spend very little time really paying attention to the quality of those conversations, which in turn means paying real attention to the quality of our listening.*

Continuing our drive to the bedrock understanding, what then accounts for effective conversation? In large part, the work that Peter and his colleagues have done suggests that one of the defining aspects of how people collaborate with one another is their capacity for and stances toward listening. How we listen to each other plays a powerful role in shaping our communication, which determines our effectiveness as a team, which in turn guides the overall success of our firm. So, through rigorous empirical inquiry, a group of Management scholars at brainy, Vulcan MIT determine that, actually, one of the core foundations of effective organizations is the quality of listening. And thus, we find ourselves at the end of this line of robust research at a very touchy-feely place. Peter argues that to improve the quality of conversations, the main thing individuals have control over is improving the quality of our own listening.

Emotions are bound up in how we listen and how we are heard, and there is no way around that if we want to lead effective organizations. So, with that, we need to talk about listening.

FOUR FIELDS OF LISTENING

Otto Sharmer is one of Peter's colleagues at the Sloan School of Management, and another organizational behavior researcher interested in how people communicate and in the interplay between personal growth and collective achievement. One of the models that he developed with Peter Senge is called the four fields of listening, which represents four typical ways that people listen to one another.

The first field of listening we might think of as "barely listening." You probably can readily recognize the qualities of barely listening in your students and colleagues. Otto Sharmer calls this "downloading," and it involves listening without attention to the speaker, mostly listening for facts and perspectives that confirm our worldview or offer some new

information. This kind of "listening" doesn't attend much to the ideas of the conversation partner; often we are just thinking about what we want to say while waiting for the other person to pause. The conversations that emerge from this kind of listening tend to be polite, uncontroversial, and highly deferential to social norms. MIT professor Chris Argys, another of Peter and Otto's collaborators, called this "talking nice."

Past barely listening is objective listening: when the listener is attending to the content of speech from a speaker. Here, listeners are acting like a kind of recording device, taking in what is said from others. One virtue of objective listening is that differences start to emerge in conversation. Conversations where people are barely listening have a kind of bland, sameness to them: you've probably been to some dinner parties or receptions characterized by a room full of people who are barely listening. People become more candid as they adopt more objective listening approaches, and the differences in perspectives that emerge can enrich discussion. But when people are serious about hearing and airing different perspectives, that can quickly lead into emotionally risky territory. People express themselves candidly, regarding each other's facts but without regard to each other's feelings or perspectives. Chris Argys called this "talking tough."

A common dysfunction of organizations is to oscillate between barely listening and objective listening, between talking nice and talking tough. Conversations start out polite, and people express only a socially acceptable range of opinions, and they minimize differences. Important issues don't get addressed, different perspectives are not aired or not heard, and conversations get boring. Eventually, someone gets frustrated at this situation and declares that there are really issues that need to be addressed. They become candid and direct. This is stressful. People's feelings get hurt. The group can't sustain the emotional tension of the conversation, and they shift back to talking nice. This cycle can continue, quite unproductively, for a long time in organizations.

Different fields, different organizations, and different cultures will have their own variations on this dysfunctional cycle of talking nice and talking tough. My hunch is that many people who work in K–12 schools will recognize "talking nice" quite readily. We have our own classrooms to retreat to, and instead of escalating conversations into talking tough, we can just go back into our own rooms. Of course, there are some virtues of polite organizations, but confronting real challenges directly, candidly, and head-on is not typically one of them. (My MIT students reading this book will recognize talking tough as a common dysfunction of software engineering teams and organizations.)

Beyond objective listening is empathetic listening, where the listener is trying to account for the identity and perspective of the speaker. Here, the listener isn't just a recording device trying to get the facts of what is being said. Instead, they are trying to quiet their own assumptions, their agendas, and that urgent desire to respond, clarify, or debate, to really try to hear what is being said from the speaker's perspective. In empathetic listening, we try to attend to the reasoning, perspectives, and assumptions of the speaker, and we wonder, "How does she see and understand what she's saying?" Empathetic listening calls for a great deal of curiosity. It sparks questions for the speaker like "How do you interpret that? How did that make you feel? What is your perspective on what you have just shared?"

The crucial difference between objective listening and empathetic listening is that in objective listening, I'm filtering the speaker's words through my own assumptions and perspectives. In empathetic listening, I'm doing my level best to set my own assumptions aside and to really try to understand what another person is saying from their vantage point. Since these conversations often happen across various lines of differences—class, race, power, gender, and so forth—part of doing this work is recognizing what assumptions I have about these differences and how they shape my listening. Ideally, this kind of listening doesn't foster talking nice or talking tough, but, rather, reflective conversation. It's at this point that groups start to feel like their collaborations are taking off in positive new directions.

Now, when you sit in a room full of people trying to collaborate, there is so much that's outside of your control. Oftentimes, we don't get to set the agenda, we can't control how people are listening, we can't dictate what people say, and we can't set the course of the conversation. I find it quite empowering to recognize that at any moment, there is one thing that we can have full control over: how we bring ourselves to the conversation. **We can always choose how we listen.** When we do our level best to listen empathetically, we can lighten and enlighten the conversation, and we can model that practice to others. When enough people listen empathetically, our teams shift away from talking tough and talking nice and toward empathetic conversation. None of this is magic beans: you can listen empathetically, the people around you can be jerks, and things can stay the same. But to me, it's a source of strength and confidence that in any conversation—in any moment in any collaboration—I have a stance that I can adopt that can help point a group in the right direction.

There is a fourth level of listening, past reflective conversation, that Peter describes as dialogue:

> *[Dialogue] is a very old word. It's a Greek word—"dia" means through; "log" comes from the Greek logos, meaning flow of meaning through—dialogos, the Greek root of the word "dialogue." The listening that allows this to occur is difficult to characterize. It's very well understood in the performing arts. In music, people will talk about being in the flow. In theater, in dance, whenever*

(Continued)

What Is the Collaborative Innovation Cycle? ● **193**

people are performing together, I guarantee you they know this distinction. Here, the whole is listening to the whole, so to speak.

It's the conversation where something new really emerges that wasn't there before. People in the world of innovation put a great deal of stock in this, because why have a meeting? Why collaborate unless something really new emerges that would not have emerged if we had continued to do things in the way we've traditionally done them?

I find Peter's words here quite inspiring, and I always chuckle to think that they come from nerds and data crunchers at the MIT

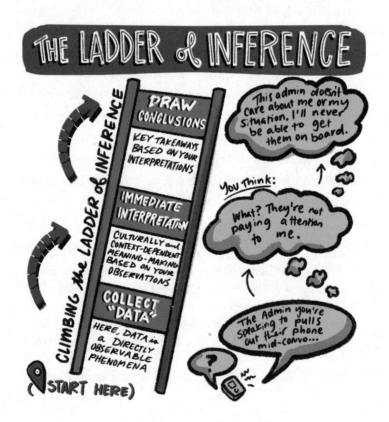

Sloan School of Management. Where does innovation come from? High-functioning, forward-thinking organizations. What makes organizations succeed? Competent teams. What makes teams work? Effective conversations. What is the source of effective conversation? Empathetic listening. In this model, our capacity to work together with other people to launch innovation, to make schools better, and to build new futures depends enormously on something so simple, so ubiquitous, so utterly under our control: how we listen to others.

TOOLS FOR BETTER LISTENING: THE LADDER OF INFERENCE

It's all well and good to recommend that you listen empathetically, but how do you do it? I have a few exercises that you can do to sharpen your listening, your collaboration, and your working together through ups and downs. One of the things that I most enjoy about working with fellow educators is that we tend to have an abiding faith in everyone's ability to improve. What we do all day is help people be better versions of themselves! Listening, like anything else, is a skill, a stance, a practice that can be improved.

I've referenced the Ladder of Inference throughout this book, especially any time I've discussed low-inference observations, like in looking at student work or with instructional rounds. The Ladder of Inference emerges from research in anthropology, where researchers tried to visit cultures very different from their own and to understand those cultures as participants in those cultures understood them, not from the perspective of the anthropologist's home culture. The Ladder of Inference has three basic steps, and they correspond to the phases with which we experience and understand the world around us.

The bottom rung of the Ladder is data. This data is not statistical data, but instead is everything that we hear, see, touch, and experience. Imagine your body and self as a recording device, just taking things in.

The middle rung is immediate interpretation. As data comes into our consciousness, it is entirely natural, and in many respects essential, to be interpreting that data. We interpret that data through the lens of our beliefs, experiences, faith, culture, history, ideology, and our sense of self. Doing this feels utterly natural. However, our interpretations can easily be quite wrong.

For instance, in the United States, nodding is generally considered a gesture of agreement. If you are talking with someone from the United States, and you observe that the head of your conversation partner is moving up and down, a very reasonable interpretation is that they agree with you. However, if you speak with someone from Japan, and you see their head moving up and down, it would be quite incorrect to make that same assumption and interpretation. In Japan, nodding during a conversation is a signal of attention— "I hear you, I hear you"—not of agreement. In Japan, you can politely nod steadily throughout a conversation in which you are attentive but totally disagree.

In the third rung of the Ladder of Inference, people draw conclusions based on their immediate interpretations. After seeing someone nod, and assuming that nodding is a sign of agreement, you proceed in the conversation to cement that agreement or move forward based on that agreement. The phrase "jumping to conclusions" refers to the very fast trips that we often take up this ladder: trusting our data collection and immediate interpretations without self-reflection in order to draw conclusions.

The Ladder of Inference reminds us to slow down and to be deliberate at each of these three stages. We have better data in conversations when we are actively listening. When we stop thinking about what we are going to say next, and we really pay attention to our conversation partner, we have better data about what they say and how they say it. As anyone with scientific training has learned, quieting and restraining our assumptions is another way to get better data collection. Of course, total objectivity is impossible, but we can develop a practice of trying to encounter data on its own terms before we interpret it. In conversations, we can listen to people and really try to understand what they said before we move to the next steps. "Let me see if I have heard you correctly," followed by restating what your conversation partner just said, is one way to get better data from listening. The practice of "low-inference observation" is the deliberate practice of gathering data before making interpretations.

At the level of interpretation, we can make several moves to listen and communicate better. We can try to deliberately quiet our own interpretations and attend to our biases. We can be curious about what alternative interpretations might be possible to a set of data, and we can be particularly curious about the assumptions and interpretations our conversation partners might have, especially partners from different backgrounds or with different perspectives. We can be explicit about our assumptions, and we can ask for clarification. "I'm seeing you nod your head, so I'm thinking that you agree with what I've just said. Is that right?"

It's through this process that we can come to better conclusions. Another way to describe this process is that **when we jump to conclusions, we treat our conclusions as data; we treat our interpretations of a situation as the facts of a situation**. When we deliberately separate the facts of a situation from our conclusions about the situation, we are better positioned to form a common ground of shared facts and data with our conversation partners. We are also better positioned to recognize the very diverse interpretations and conclusions that can exist in a group around those shared facts.

As you become proficient at attending to your own assumptions and quieting them as best you can, you will find that this low-inference approach to observation and questioning is valuable throughout the design process. I'm emphasizing it here in working through the challenges of collaboration, but it's also an invaluable approach in the Discover phase of Design Thinking for Leading and Learning, where we are trying to understand how community members and stakeholders understand their challenges and their world. It's valuable in peer learning in the Cycle of Experiment and Peer Learning, when we use Looking at Student Work or Instruction Rounds to see what our colleagues are doing or to invite them in our own classrooms. So much of design is doing our level best to get outside of our own heads and perspectives, and the Ladder of Inference is a valuable thinking tool in that important work.

ADDRESSING DISAGREEMENT THROUGH A BIAS TO ACTION

I hope you are now convinced of the potential of better listening to improve communication and collaboration. Effective listening will make you more aware of the diverse perspectives of your colleagues and teammates and it will create opportunities to hear more ideas and explore those new frontiers. It will surface important disagreements and differences.

Sadly, listening will not resolve those disagreements. Good leadership is not erasing disagreements. Good leadership involves acknowledging differences, making space for diverse perspectives, honoring the inevitability of conflict, and helping teams continue to work together through all that tumult.

In an orchestra, people have all kinds of different beliefs about what makes for beautiful music: different preferences, different warm-up routines, different approaches to playing their instruments or engaging a song. These differences are not all resolved before the conductor raises their baton; they exist while the orchestra starts playing and comes together to make beautiful music. This concept can be very freeing. We can disagree on lots of things, and we inevitably will. We need some agreement about what good outcomes would be in each situation, and all the tools of bringing people together can help generate some of that agreement about goals. But we don't need agreement to have alignment: the disposition to work together toward common goals.

Throughout this book, I've argued that a bias to action can be a powerful stance toward more effective design. There is energy in starting new initiatives and improvements, and we understand our environments in new ways as we do the work of trying to improve them. Similarly, a second way to address disagreement, after accepting the inevitability of disagreement and working toward alignment instead, is to move forward in doing the work. Sometimes, it's simply enough to get started together, to build together, and hopefully to get some wins together. As people see success and progress despite their disagreements, they are better able to accept differences.

Sometimes disagreements are fundamental to getting to work: disagreements about desired outcomes, important areas of focus, or key methods for getting work done. These are harder to work through, but again a bias to action is one way to address these disagreements. In the world of scholarly research, the psychologist Daniel Kahneman has proposed "adversarial collaboration" as one method for addressing disagreements.[3] Essentially, the people with a substantive disagreement come to a procedural agreement to work together to design some kind of experiment or test that would shed light on their disagreement.

For instance, several years into the pandemic, as student test scores plummeted, policymakers came to two different conclusions about how to address the unfinished learning from emergency school closures. One strategy was to try to ramp up learning time through more tutoring, summer school, and extended learning time.

A second strategy was to focus on community, relationship building, and reducing the complexity of schooling so that students felt healthier and stronger as they engaged in their day-to-day schooling. If a school team is paralyzed by disagreement about which path to pursue, one approach is to agree to conduct experiments along the lines of both approaches. Partisans of each perspective should help the other team build the best possible version of each approach. Teams should agree on what kind of evidence will be examined to validate each hypothesis. And then, ideally, both groups agree to have more intensive future work be guided by which approach appears most effective.

To do that, you'll need to make a commitment to measure how your efforts are progressing.

MEASURING PROGRESS AND ADJUSTING

Assessment is essential to improving and sustaining innovation. The only way new innovations lead to better outcomes is to try things, evaluate them, examine the results a disciplined way, and then see what you can learn about improving. Some of the things we try don't work at all, and nearly everything we try doesn't work right away.

Now, unfortunately, many public school educators feel like assessment has been weaponized as a bludgeon against teachers rather than as a tool to support them. That makes it much harder to enshrine professional formative assessment as the critical component of innovation that it is. But all that politics and baggage doesn't change the fact that if we want to improve, we need to be able to look at what we're doing in a systematic way.

I have visited many schools that are multiple years into a technology initiative or other innovation program, and most of them cannot provide systematic evidence about the effect of the program. It is a very tiny number that can make reasonable claims about the effect of these initiatives on student learning, even though student learning is the entire point of these new efforts.

And I get it: everyone is busy. It's very uncomfortable asking tough questions, and it's hard when we learn that our newfound efforts aren't landing where we hope. But there is no way around looking closely at new efforts and closely examining whether they are really working.

So, my advice on measuring progress and adjusting boils down to two simple messages. First, get started. Whatever new initiative you have going, commit to gathering some new kind of evidence about whether it's working as you intended. If you are swamped, and you probably are, there are relatively simple, time-efficient ways to begin assessing new programs. Don't let the perfect be the enemy of the good.

The second message is related: assessment is more about disciplined common sense than any special technical expertise. You can go and get a PhD in program evaluation, and if you have someone on staff with some technical assessment skills, then put them to work. But my goal in this section is to demonstrate that smart educators like you can come up with great ideas for how to begin assessing new initiatives. The hard part is more about getting started and making time than it is about figuring out exactly what to do.

KEY PRINCIPLES FOR MEASURING PROGRESS AND ADJUSTING

The first principle is to have a bias to action: get started. Find one person who has been touched—or should have been touched—by your latest initiative and ask them how it's going. When the conversation is over, pat yourself on the back: you've started to measure progress and adjust. Keep going.

Then, as initiatives become larger and more developed, collect more rigorous evidence of efficacy. For smaller initiatives or for any early-phase initiative, start by gathering people's subjective impressions through interviews, surveys, and focus groups. Seek out more objective data—from student work, assessments, and tests—as your improvement efforts become more developed, more complete, or closer to the shift from innovation to typical practice.

Be deliberate about soliciting feedback from diverse sources, not the easiest ones. The students, parents, and colleagues who are easiest to talk to—the ones who complete a survey first or raise their hands all the time to participate in interviews and feedback—often are not representative of your whole school community. Who doesn't speak English? Who already expressed opposition to the effort? Which students usually miss school, or which parents can't often come in during a school day? If you aren't gathering data from these folks on the margins, then you aren't evaluating how your programs are affecting some of your most important community members.

One great tool for ensuring that you are talking to diverse people or examining diverse student work is randomization. It is pretty simple to use, and it is a powerful way to examine a sample of people who are likely to be representative of a larger group. For instance, let's say you were running a schoolwide initiative on "eliciting learner knowledge," the art and practice of taking more time to understand student thinking before offering feedback or corrections. If all of the teachers in your school are participating in this initiative, then ideally you'd be able to walk into any classroom and see evidence of behaviors like wait time, probing questions, or making student thinking visible. Before choosing to visit a few classrooms, assign every teacher a number, and then generate a random list of numbers (random.org is a great website for this). Visit the teachers in the order dictated by the random list, and you'll be less likely to wander only into the rooms of your closest colleagues who will validate your feelings by fully participating in your initiative. You'll be more likely to see what's really happening in your school.

GATHERING EVIDENCE FROM ARTIFACTS OF LEARNING

Student learning is the primary purpose of schools.

That's an obvious statement, but it's also often forgotten or set aside. It is entirely normal and natural for the logistical complexities of schools to so completely overwhelm the attention of administrators, and sometimes teachers, that we confuse making schools work for making students learn.

One of my favorite illustrations of this principle was at a tech conference several years ago where an IT leader was asked to explain why a school had chosen iPad tablets as their device for a one-to-one program. He talked about their long battery life, the ease of carrying them around, and how they no longer had power cords crisscrossing the classroom. Now, I am all for workplace safety, and I certainly don't want teachers to trip. But these simply are not the right reasons to justify an instructional tool. The first and last justification for technology needs to be student learning. If we can't explain to students, parents, colleagues, boards, trustees, and community members how new tools lead to better learning, then we shouldn't be spending money on new tools.

The best place to look for evidence of learning is student work: in classrooms, on homework, and for projects. If student work isn't improving as the result of a new effort or initiative, why do it? Even our efforts at things like building community, addressing trauma, strengthening home–school relationships—these efforts have value, but they also ought to pay dividends in terms of student learning.

I discussed a bit about looking at student work in previous chapters, and the advice there still holds. Let me share here one of my favorite examples of measuring progress and adjusting at the school level rather than the classroom level.

In the 2000s, Bud Hunt was the IT director in Colorado's St. Vrain School District, and he wrote his master's thesis on a school-wide blogging initiative. In the 2000s, Web 2.0—things like blogs, wikis, and other participatory media—were heralded as important innovations in school. Bud helped his school set up a schoolwide blogging infrastructure where every teacher and student got access to their own personal blog. He was particularly interested in helping students develop their own voice and perspective on these issues. But he didn't just set up the blog and trust that good things would follow. As part of his master's thesis, he conducted a study about whether the actual writing students did on their blogs aligned with his hopes. (Are there teachers or educators in your school working on a master's thesis? Put them to work like Bud!)

Here, briefly, is what Bud did:

- He took a sample of all his school's blog posts.

- He read them.

- He categorized them.

- He drew some conclusions about the kinds of learning taking place based on that analysis.

In simplifying Bud's thesis, I don't want to minimize the work that he did. But I do want to highlight that it wasn't rocket science; it was the kind of action research project—research where a teacher investigates a new initiative in progress—that any team of educators in a school or district could tackle. His work is systematic, not complex, and his results are compelling and troubling. Basically, Bud found that most blogging activity was either teacher-centered content delivery or the kind of simple hub-and-spoke interactions typically found in classrooms, where a teacher asks a question, a kid responds, and a teacher evaluates. In general, Bud didn't find young people finding a voice, developing an identity as a blogger, or pursuing topics and conversations with passion and interest. He found them producing perfunctory answers to the same kinds of questions they got in class. His research raises some important questions for the teachers in his district about blogging practice specifically and technology-mediated collaborative learning more broadly.

There is so much here that Bud does right in his research project that makes it a model for other educators. First, Bud doesn't try to read everything that has ever been produced on blogs in his district; he takes a sample. He then investigates that sample in a systematic, but not overly complicated, way. Basically, he looked at a pilot set of blog posts and developed a taxonomy of about 10 "purposes" of a blog post, and then he measured the distribution of those purposes in the full sample. In his analysis, he's also fearless in confronting what his findings suggest about student learning opportunities. He found that blogging online looked too much like the kinds of writing that students did offline, and he challenged his colleagues to embrace the possibilities of the new medium. It's a tough message that Bud has to deliver to his fellow educators in his district. But it's very difficult to imagine that community of educators getting any better without facing up to the analysis that Bud has done. This kind of assessment data gives teachers something concrete to use as they build a conversation about how they can make the actual results of an innovation line up better with their hopes and ideals.

GATHERING EVIDENCE FROM PEOPLE

Looking at student work is time-consuming. There can also be long cycles between starting an instructional improvement initiative, changing instructional practices, and seeing the fruits of better student learning. So along with student work, innovation launchers can track the results of their efforts by talking to people. I already introduced interviewing approaches in the Discover and Try phases of Design Thinking for Leading and Learning, and we can go deeper here.

The canonical way that qualitative researchers learn from other people is through interviews. Identify a random sample of important stakeholders connected to a new initiative: students, faculty, parents, and so on. Come up with a list of questions that you will try to ask everyone, and a list of follow-up prompts that will help you understand a new initiative. You don't have to ask everyone the exact same questions, but it can be helpful to explore common themes across interviews.

Whenever possible, ask general, open-ended questions about a domain before specific questions about an initiative. You only have one chance in an interview to find out what's top of mind for people; once you start asking questions, you subtly shift the way people think about a topic. For instance, if Bud Hunt were to interview students about his blogging initiative, he might start with a question like "What kinds of writing are you doing in your classes?" before asking the question "What kind of writing do you do on your blogs?" or "Do you think the blogging initiative is effective for your learning?" The latter two questions are good ones, but as soon as you ask about a specific initiative, you've set the frame. If interview participants respond to the open-ended question about writing by talking about blogs, then you know something important about how people are thinking about the initiative. If people only talk about your innovation when you directly ask about it, then that is telling you something as well.

When you want to know how lots of people think about a topic, then surveys can be a valuable tool. Surveys are basically structured interviews in which the interviewer cannot vary the questions asked or adjust the interview based on participant responses. In many dimensions, they are less precise and comprehensive instruments than interviews, but they have the virtue of being distributed more widely and easily than setting up lots of interviews.

The rules for surveys are similar to those for interviews: ask open-ended questions first and focus on more specific questions later. Remember that people who readily respond to surveys are probably systematically different than those who don't respond. It may be more valuable to identify a random sample of 100 students or parents and to do everything possible to get them to complete a survey through extra time, incentives, and personal requests than it is to send a survey to everyone and simply look at the 200 survey responses from people who decide to respond. In other words, a smaller number of representative responses may be better than a larger number of biased ones.

If you ask anyone who has designed a survey, they will tell you that people are shockingly good at interpreting survey questions in unexpected ways. Even the simplest questions can open the door to all kinds of misinterpretations. Before fielding an important survey, have a few representative participants take a pilot version of the survey, and ask them lots of questions about how they interpreted the items on the survey.

As you combine all these techniques of learning from people, remember to not let the perfect be the enemy of the good. When you start a new instructional initiative, just whip up an exit ticket for when you try a new approach and get a little bit of feedback from students about what they thought of the new lesson, approach, or technique. As you scale up an initiative to work in more classrooms, or more thoroughly throughout a curriculum, you should then interview or survey more people about their experience, bring in other educators to observe practice, and ultimately look closely at student work. But don't be so paralyzed by the possibilities of assessment that you don't do anything. As with everything else, start small and build up, devoting more time to assessing and adjusting as your programs and innovation become more fleshed out, more expansive, or more complex.

USING ASSESSMENT TO REVITALIZE INITIATIVES AND TO GET UNSTUCK

As I've worked with many schools about their innovation initiatives, I've seen that it's very common and normal for those initiatives to lose their way over time. Questions of teaching and learning get overwhelmed by questions of logistics, and the sense of purpose and mission gets overwhelmed by the urgency of maintenance. That's all normal.

One way to help innovation get unstuck is to ask the question, "How do we know that this is working?" That question will provoke conversations about evidence and assessment; it's not uncommon for a surprising follow-up question to emerge: "Well, what were we trying to do?" It's all too easy in the implementation of innovation to lose sight of its original purpose. Doing good assessment and measurement requires going back to those questions or mission. We can't develop good program assessments if we don't know what it is a new initiative was trying to accomplish. For initiatives that feel listless or stuck, conversations about evidence and assessment can help people return to the reasons behind new efforts.

For a period in my career, I found these conversations very frustrating, but over time I've realized that our callings and passions are often defined by the conversations we are willing to have over and over again. If you are serious about helping schools get better at teaching and learning, then it doesn't really matter that schools often aren't that great at measuring progress and adjusting. As we do with young people, we need to meet adults where they are. People should have kept the mission in the forefront of their innovation, but if they haven't, then today is the best day to go back to it. People should be measuring progress and adjusting throughout their improvement efforts, but as the saying goes, if yesterday was the best day to start using assessment in continuous improvement, then today is the second-best day to start.

CONCLUSION

Whenever we come to the end of a cycle, it's time again to start thinking about what the next loop might look like. Remembering where you started can be very helpful in figuring out where to go next after a period of measuring progress and adjusting.

Maybe you started your Collaborative Innovation Cycle with very loose alignment and with limited coherence. Maybe your Monday-type efforts at getting to work stumbled a bit, and maybe your assessment efforts revealed that people still have disagreements and misalignment that are limiting your sense of shared purpose. That's all normal and part of the process; hopefully you have kept your experiments light and fast enough that you learned those important lessons without spending too much time and effort. If things are rocky, go back to ideas from Bringing People Together Around Ideas They Care About. Try to identify the high points and best examples of alignment from your efforts, clarify the overlapping goals that can build toward shared purpose, and use those conversations to get started on another round of iterative efforts. If it's interpersonal conflicts that are holding back your progress or making moving forward difficult, think about how you can make space to really listen to the concerns that people are bringing to the table. Nothing is a foolproof strategy for working together through conflicts, but making sure people are really heard is one potent place to start.

If your experiments did seem to be bringing about a convergence on alignment and shared mission, then keep going forward. If you had the right shared outcome but the wrong approach, return to Refining a Vision. If you seem to be heading in the right direction with the right innovation, then use everything you've learned about human-centered design to keep iterating and refining. If you've been cycling through lots of iterations, and getting positive vibes from teachers, students, and stakeholders, but you aren't really sure if what you are doing is advancing your objectives and outcomes, it may be time to slow down on improving the innovation and spend more time measuring progress so you can do some good, evidence-informed adjusting.

Hopefully, the Collaborative Innovation Cycle offers a framework for bringing together more people in greater alignment to do bigger things in your community. In the next chapter, I share some of the tools that my colleagues and I have developed for enriching your collaboration, finding shared vision out of an array of personal visions, listening and working together, and assessing your progress as you move forward.

TOOLS AND STRATEGIES FOR THE COLLABORATIVE INNOVATION CYCLE

The Collaborative Innovation Cycle builds on the Cycle of Experiment and Peer Learning and Design Thinking for Leading and Learning in three ways. First, as the name implies, it emphasizes the collaborative, and, ideally, schoolwide nature of the innovation process. If the Design Thinking ideas in this book help you start a single classroom experiment, Collaborative Innovation is more about guiding teams, departments, schools, and districts. That work starts by Bringing People Together Around Ideas They Care About. As you bring people together and collaborate, there will be conflict. As you make changes, there will be loss. That's inevitable. So, the second area for growth in the Collaborative Innovation Cycle is around Working Together Through Ups and Downs. Then as your innovation work develops, you will need to get serious about whether what you are doing is really working, and that requires a third new piece: Measuring Progress and Adjusting.

Since collaboration is the centerpiece of this work, in this chapter, I share a series of activities that you can conduct with your colleagues. They are all field-tested efforts that I've run dozens of times with in-person groups and with many thousands of people online. Some topics in the previous chapter may have felt abstract, such as creating a shared vision, listening more carefully, or assessing new initiatives. I hope that these activities will make those areas feel more concrete. There are many of these activities that you could do by yourself, but as much as possible, I'd encourage you to collaborate with other colleagues in your community.

ACTIVITIES FOR BRINGING PEOPLE TOGETHER AROUND IDEAS THEY CARE ABOUT

As Peter Senge explains, shared vision is the weaving together of diverse personal visions. When educators come together to work toward better schools, they typically start from their own sense of what constitutes a powerful learning environment. These individual imaginations provide important fuel, motivation, and grounding for collaborative efforts. Asking people to reflect on their vision of a powerful learning environment is a tried-and-true way of starting or revitalizing work with schools and educator teams.

The framing text for each of the following activities is the kind of language that I use to present the activities to teams of educators. If you are doing these activities on your own, you can read the text as an invitation from me to you. If you are leading these activities with your colleagues, you might think about how you could take the themes and ideas from these introductions and adapt them in your own voice to make them relevant to your personal context.

VISIONS FOR A POWERFUL LEARNING ENVIRONMENT

I view the process of launching change as an exciting and inspiring opportunity to make teaching and learning better. Starting that improvement process begins with a critical question: What does "better" look like for you? We can start answering that question by considering our personal vision of what excellent teaching and learning looks like for teachers, students, and other stakeholders. I'm not saying that you can turn your school into an educational utopia overnight, but this is the time to "dream big" and let those dreams influence your work going forward. Each of these personal visions is going to be source material and fuel for developing a shared vision.

1. Take a moment to think about the most powerful learning environment you've experienced as a student.

2. Think about a powerful learning environment you've observed but not necessarily participated in.

3. Now think about the most compelling and powerful learning environment you've created as an educator or helped create/enable as an administrator.

What did these environments feel like? What did they sound like? What did they look like? What were students doing in these settings? What were teachers doing?

Take 10 to 15 minutes for people to write a description of their vision of a powerful learning environment. It might be one particular moment from one special classroom or place, or it might be a compilation or medley of different learning environments. Each person can write, draw, or express their powerful learning environment however they like. As you wrap up, give each person time to highlight the three most important elements of their vision.

If you're working with a group, after each individual writes down their personal description, post them somewhere visible to everyone. If you have few enough people, have folks share their contributions. If you are doing this with a whole faculty, you might have people read the visions posted on walls or break into groups to discuss a sample.

Now compare the ideas. What are the commonalities? Do the commonalities align with the school, district, and community values? What are the differences and why? Having people discuss where their powerful learning environments differ helps you to better understand each other as educators.

Once you have considered the key elements of your powerful learning environment, create an image that evokes your vision of a powerful learning environment. You could make a collage or drawing or take a photo. You could also edit or annotate an image that already exists. Explain how your image represents your idea of a powerful learning environment and how it connects to the three important elements that you defined.

Now that you've got your vision, get out in your school community and ask people what they think a powerful learning environment looks like, and share your thoughts with others. Talk with a student about what a powerful learning environment means to them. Compare and contrast your idea of a powerful learning environment with your students'. Ask a colleague in your department or in a separate department. After you've had a few conversations about these powerful learning environments, reflect on what you've learned. How might people in the same school or district differ on what a powerful learning environment looks like? How might their ideas be similar? Who or what influences how an educator develops a vision of powerful learning?

As educators, we spend so much of our time keeping schools running and putting out fires. Stepping back from the day to day and focusing our ideals is a valuable way to refocus on our priorities, remember our motivations, and establish the "Someday" vision that can guide our Someday/Monday work.

FOUR QUESTIONS FOR INNOVATION

This activity is meant to reveal the strengths and values of your school community and to help imagine how new innovations can build on those strengths.

Supplies needed:

- Large sticky notes, at least 10–15 per person (it's important to get ones about as big as an index card, so everyone can see what is written)

- Markers

- Poster board/whiteboard

Instructions:

1. Set up a room with four places (corners, walls, tables, etc.) where lots of sticky notes can be displayed and moved around. Ideally, the spaces would be big enough that several people can cluster around each of the four spaces at once. Label each of the four places with one of the four questions below.

2. Make sure each person in the room has at least 10–15 sticky notes. Explain that you will ask people a series of four questions, and they should write down their answers to these questions with one idea per sticky note. Emphasize that you're not looking for the "right" answers to these questions (like what would appear on the school or district's website), but that people should write what is most real and important to them. As people finish writing down their thoughts, have them bring the sticky notes up to the first corner labeled with the first question. Then move on to each of the next questions in turn. Here are the four questions:

   - What would you say are some of the signature strengths of our school or district? Think about the things that everyone (parents, students, and faculty) is most proud of. When you think about your school or district, what is the thing that gets you smiling? When someone new comes to interview at your school or district and asks "Why should I work here?," how would you answer them?

- What are the learning outcomes for the students in our school or district that are most important to you? When you think about the skills, knowledge, and character qualities of graduates from your district, what are the qualities that you most care about?

- What are the major initiatives of any kind that are going on in our district right now? If asked "What are you working on? What are you trying to improve?," what would teachers and administrators say? What are the main things, whether it's districtwide or happening in one or a couple of schools?

- The most promising potential innovation for improving teaching and learning in your school is _____. You could spend days thinking about this, but just capture the first few thoughts that appear in your mind.

Whenever I conduct this activity, these first three questions are always the same. The fourth question should be tailored toward the innovation that you and your colleagues are exploring. For instance, for districts that are working on technology-related innovation, a good final question might be:

- The most promising use of technology in the classroom is _____.

In a district working on differentiated instruction, or response to intervention, or something similar, the question might be:

- The most promising strategies for differentiating instruction for all learners is_____.

If you aren't yet sure of the direction of your next area of focus, then you might use something like:

- The most promising potential innovation for improving teaching and learning in our school is

  _____.

3 As people finish posting the final notes, have everyone start a gallery walk around the room. I usually start this phase with a little speech:

"In every group of people there are those who, when faced with sticky notes, feel an uncontrollable desire to organize them. If that is you, my friend, then now is your time to shine."

Or find another way to encourage folks to go around the room, organize the sticky notes into clusters, and then identify commonalities, differences, surprises, and other patterns.

Debrief:

4 Looking at your answers for the first three questions, find the commonalities and the differences. Discuss why your answers might be similar (does it come from a framework that the whole district has adopted?) or different (e.g., a high school might want college-ready students while that might not be a focus for an elementary school). The initiatives wall is often a powerful barometer for how a school or district is doing. A wall with many, many initiatives is usually a place with too many mandates and too little focus. A wall where all the Post-it Notes repeat the same few themes is a good indicator of a school or district where people are already in sync with each other.

5   Celebrate. Most school communities have lots of answers
    to the first two questions that ought to be a source of pride.
    There are usually common themes that reflect shared under-
    standing and purpose. During the debrief, it's worth taking
    a few minutes to appreciate some of the best ideas that are
    most widely shared. Again, in the day-to-day hustle of schools,
    we can often lose sight of the importance of celebrating our
    accomplishments.

6   Punchline: Of course, the conversations that you have
    throughout your debrief will be particular to the colleagues
    whom you are working with. But in every group that I work
    with, I always make sure to end with this crucial point: the
    answers to the fourth question need to connect to the
    answers to the first three questions. New innovations need to
    build upon the existing strengths, values, and initiatives of a
    community. When new innovations feel like "one more thing"
    to a community, it's hard for them to garner support. If a

school has been working on improving differentiated instruction for several years, then the new technology initiative should be seen as a way to extend and improve that initiative. When you start down the path to change, it will be easier and more fruitful to engage with others in your school if you have a good understanding of how your initiative fits within your school context.

ASSET MAPPING

The Four Questions for Innovation should help point your community towards ideas that you care about. This next exercise, Asset Mapping, is about identifying allies and collaborators who are already supporting school improvement efforts and can aid you in your new innovation work. An asset map is a visual representation of the valuable resources around you and how they connect.

- Think about a big task or project that you have recently completed where you work. Who did you work with to accomplish your goals? Who was especially helpful? Start a list of these people.

- Identify various stakeholders such as students, parents, administrators, and community members, and consider how these people participate in, influence, and shape new initiatives. Write some notes for each person. Rather than just writing "support personnel," we recommend being as specific as possible. Think about including specific people or titles, like "sixth-grade technology integration specialist."

- Take your list and create a map that shows connections between the helpful, supportive people you identified. From

ASSET MAPPING

PROBLEM of PRACTICE: HOW to ENGAGE QUIET STUDENTS in CLASS?

SPACES
- LUNCH WITH OTHER 6TH GRADE TEACHERS
- ENGLISH TEACHER MEETING

VALUES
- EXPERIMENTATION
- ENGAGING ALL STUDENTS
- UDL

RESOURCES
- FLEXIBLE CLASSROOM SET-UP
- CLASSROOM OBSERVATIONS

TEACHERS
+ SUPPORTIVE COLLABORATORS
− NOT ENOUGH TIME IN THE DAY!

ME! (MISS MILLS, ENGLISH TEACHER)
+ WILLING to TRY NEW THINGS (SOCRATIC SEMINAR?)
- WELL CONNECTED
− NEED HELP to EVALUATE if NEW THINGS WORK WELL

STUDENTS
+ CURIOUS · DIVERSE INTERESTS
− TIRED at the END of a LONG DAY · WORRIED ABOUT GRADES

ADMIN
+ RESPONSIVE to NEEDS + REQUESTS · SUPPORTIVE of FACULTY
− OVERCOMMITTED

your notes, identify key players who may be especially important to engage as you start to envision change. Your network map should help illuminate the ecosystem of your school; you'll likely see that you have more allies than you thought.

There may be specific conditions of your environment that make starting a new initiative easier. For example, if you eventually decide that the innovation you want to focus on involves reinvigorating the arts in your school, it's a great resource to be in a city with numerous art museums or a vibrant street art scene. Now that you have created a first draft of an asset map with all the people who might be able to support new innovation initiatives, add to the map by including other community resources:

- Ask yourself, What is present in the community that could help you to address the key innovation initiative in your school? Why are they strong assets? How do the assets relate to one another? Some examples of assets:

  - *Community values/beliefs*: Do your innovation initiatives align with any goals or missions of your community?

  - *Community resources*: These include a wide range of things such as municipal funding or community organizations.

  - *Spaces*: This could mean actual physical spaces for meetings and other activities (e.g., your school or other community spaces) as well as online spaces such as social media groups or online learning spaces.

  - *Time*: Maybe you have some free periods each school day or flexibility regarding professional development opportunities.

  - *Personal strengths*: You are also an asset! Consider your personal strengths that make you the perfect leader to tackle innovation areas. Your skills might include enthusiasm, communication skills, respect of colleagues, willingness to try new things, perseverance, and so on.

- Use symbols and images to create your asset map. Highlight importance, type, strength of connection, and so on through shape, color, line, size.

- At the bottom or side of your map, create a legend or explanatory text paragraph regarding how to read your map.

After you've created your asset map, reflect on the process of creating the map. Was there a connection you didn't realize you had or a strength you felt was reaffirmed? What worries or concerns have you identified based on this exercise? In my experience, when educators conduct this exercise, they often walk away from the effort realizing that there are many more assets that they and their community have to draw on then they originally believed. People care deeply about their schools, and our communities are filled with talented people, special places, and important resources. Starting the process of launching innovation in schools by remembering all these assets is a way of organizing all of the strengths and people that a new initiative can build upon.

ACTIVITIES FOR REFINING A VISION AND GETTING TO WORK

EXPLORING POSSIBLE VISIONS: RIGHTBORO SCENARIOS

One way to help imagine possible futures for your school is to explore case studies of existing schools. The Rightboro Scenarios activity looks at four examples of different approaches to taking advantage of a new school building and technology investment. In this activity, participants will use a "jigsaw" method to review four different approaches to improving schools.

One of the key arguments from the activity is that the signature quality of our most effective schools is "coherence," where faculty and students have a shared vision and shared instructional language. Each of the four districts is pursuing a version of what might be called "personalized" learning that attempts to attend to the needs and interests of individual students. That's a worthy goal, but there are many different, conflicting, and even contradictory ways of pursuing that goal. The activity is also designed to highlight how education buzzwords can have very different meanings to different people. That's okay; it just means that communities need to take the time to build a shared language and understanding of new ideas and areas for innovation.

Since much of my work has been near my home in New England, the four scenarios describe a typical suburban school district in the Northeast. Even the name, "Rightboro," is a play on typical regional names: in Massachusetts we have Northboro, Southboro, Westboro, Middleboro, Attleboro, and the famous Foxboro, home of the Patriots (if you aren't from Massachusetts, trust me that the name Rightboro is hilarious). In your work, you might modify the names and details of the scenarios to align better with your own local context. All four scenarios start by describing a district building a new high school, but then each district takes their new school in a different direction.

Instructions:

The Rightboro Scenarios are best explored as a jigsaw activity, where participants spend two rounds in two different small groups.

1. In the first round, divide the participants up into either four or eight groups (or a multiple of four that fits your group size).
2. Give each group one of the four Rightboro scenarios.
   Remind participants that the scenarios are very short, and

necessarily are missing details. Have the group spend five to seven minutes writing some notes in response to the following questions:

- What seem to be the strengths of this school's approach?

- What seem to be the weaknesses of their approach?

- What are two questions you might ask to flesh this scenario out?

- If you really wanted this approach to be successful, what is one action you would prioritize?

3 Each person should become an "expert" in their scenario and be prepared to explain highlights from your discussion with others.

4 Next, "jigsaw" the participants so that they get into new small groups, where each group has someone with each of the four scenarios. Each group should respond to a new set of questions:

- What are the dimensions of difference across these scenarios? What elements are common to each scenario, but expressed differently in each?

- What are some of the pros and cons of each scenario?

- How could each scenario be considered an example of personalized learning?

- Finally, do any of the scenarios represent a plausible path forward for your school?

SCENARIOS

Rightboro is an affluent town in the suburbs of Boston with approximately 4,000 students in four elementary schools, a middle school, and a high school. The Rightboro School Board received approval for state matching funds three years ago to build a new, state-of-the-art high school facility. The new building will open this September, and it has excellent, high-speed, redundant connections to the Internet and wireless access that reaches every classroom and study space.

Scenario 1: Focus on STEM Belief/Mission: Rightboro believes that STEM fields will offer the greatest opportunities for its graduates in the decades ahead and hopes to prepare students who are familiar with design thinking, engineering principles, and project management. Rightboro's new high school will include several "maker spaces" that are outfitted with a wide variety of hand tools, building materials, electronics components, small computers like Arduinos, and larger tools such as 3D printers and laser cutters. During their freshman year, students take a combined humanities/physics class that culminates in a major class project, such as a short play performed on a set built by the class or moving dioramas of life in ancient civilizations. In subsequent years, students are encouraged to take computer science and engineering electives that focus on programming robots to complete complex tasks like cutting fruit, folding towels, or competing in obstacle courses. All classes are encouraged to offer students "20% time," where they can spend one class period a week devising projects of their own choosing for presentation at the end of the semester. Rightboro judges the success of their program by evaluating the quality of final projects from courses, electives, and independent projects, and by evaluating the number of students, especially girls and students of color, who go on to pursue STEM majors in college.

Scenario 2: Self-Pacing and Specialization Rightboro believes that every student should be able to advance through the academic curriculum at their own pace, and that they should be able to specialize in particular fields during high school. Rightboro's new high school provides a laptop for each student, and the core curriculum in English, Math, and Science is available for students online. Students spend much of their time working independently on learning modules and assignments. Each student has their own cubicle space for independent work, and they proceed at their own pace. In the core courses, the primary role for teachers is to evaluate student data from these assignments and identify students who need additional support, such as small group instruction or one-on-one tutoring. In the upper grades, students are encouraged to take online courses through partnerships with local community colleges to begin earning college credit. When certain courses are not available, students are encouraged to find MOOCs or other open online courses that fulfill their interests, and faculty work with students to help them earn credit for these courses through an "independent study" program overseen by faculty mentors. Rightboro judges the success of their program by evaluating the number of students who can enter college with advanced standing to either graduate earlier or pursue more advanced specializations.

Scenario 3: Focus on Communication Skills and Building a Portfolio Rightboro believes that successful graduates will have strong multimedia communication skills and leave school with a portfolio that vividly illustrates their learning and accomplishments. Rightboro has a one-to-one tablet program where every student has their own iPad, and students are taught to see the tablet not as a simple replacement for notebooks or textbooks, but as a powerful multimedia device for creating, editing, and publishing. In all courses, students use the iPad to document their learning: they take photographs of observations in science labs, make screencast recordings of problem-solving in math class, and publish reflective literature blogs with snippets of annotated text in English class. All classrooms have at least two Apple TVs that allow students to easily project and share their work. Every semester, courses have "capstone projects" that involve creating a summative performance of understanding, curating key assignments from throughout the semester, and publishing a reflective multimedia essay about their semester. All this work is published on a school platform, and students are also encouraged to publish their best work publicly online. Rightboro judges the success of the program by evaluating the quality of student portfolios and by Googling the names of the graduates and evaluating the character of their online footprint.

Scenario 4: Flipping the Classroom and Fostering Independent Learners Rightboro believes that successful students are independent learners who can demonstrate mastery of skills and knowledge within the core subject areas. Rightboro faculty have invested heavily in creating faculty-produced open-source video textbooks, where teachers explain core ideas in their subject areas. Classes are then run using a "flipped model" where students watch video lectures, do online activities, and read source material at home, and then come into school for discussions, projects, and assessments. Each course has a defined set of standards, and students are evaluated on the coverage and depth of mastery of those standards. Any assessment can be retaken or revised, and a student's final grade is determined by the proportion of standards mastered by the end of the semester, not the quality of work produced in developing mastery. Most classrooms are designed as "agile classrooms," with movable furniture that allows students to organize into working groups of different sizes, or to work independently. Rightboro has a "Bring-Your-Own-Device" policy where students can access the open-source video textbooks and other course materials from their own personal devices, and they are encouraged to complete assessments and do in-class activities using those same devices. Rightboro judges the success of their program by evaluating the total number of standards mastered by all graduating students as a proportion of the total number of possible standards to be mastered.

Debrief:

1. Bring the whole group back together. Have folks report out on the dimensions of difference that they identified. Some of these might include:

    - Purpose of schools and key qualities for success-ful graduates

    - Breadth or focus of the mission

    - Pedagogical approaches aligned with the focus of the school

    - Specific strategies for measuring progress

    When I do the debrief, I emphasize that one of the strengths of all four approaches is that they embody a clear set of values, and they enact those values throughout the school. Here's how I might explain this point to a group:

    "I'm glad you got a chance to explore these different scenarios, which are based on real schools that are all trying to improve learning for students in different ways. One of the things that distinguishes the four scenarios from each other is that each of those school communities has different sets of beliefs. Some of those different beliefs are about what students need to be able to do to thrive in the future. What would your community say about what the most important skills and competencies are for students to do well in the future? Each of the school communities also has different beliefs about what their strengths are and what they're good at. Your beliefs about what good learning should help students be able to do and your beliefs about what your strengths and culture should offer to students are two crucial starting points for thinking about new innovations and new directions and new visions for schools."

2. Next, ask people to reflect on how each of these schools might be doing some form of personalized learning. One of the schools tries to personalize learning by optimizing each student's trajectory through the school. Another school focuses on personalization around students' individual interests. It's important to know that the term personalized learning does not mean much unless it's defined by the school using it based on that school's beliefs, strengths, and so on. Discuss other terms that might differ depending on the setting. In your school, is there any vocabulary that might be defined differently depending on the department or the classroom? How might you correct this in your school?

One of the most common responses from educators participating in these scenarios is to want to take bits and pieces from each school and combine them. As a facilitator, I push back against this perspective. It would take years for most schools to improve any one of these approaches to teaching and learning, let alone multiple ones.

And if we look at our best schools, they tend to provide more of a coherent, focused learning experience than trying to have bits and pieces of lots of approaches but no real focus. There isn't necessarily one perfect system of schooling, but many of our best schools identify a focus and pursue that. It's not about picking one right system; it's about getting one system right.

The Rightboro Scenarios are loosely based on existing schools. Scenario 1 is inspired by project-based schools, like the High Tech High network in San Diego or Philadelphia's Science Leadership Academy. Scenario 2 is based on Village Green Academy in Rhode Island: a model that many educators found very surprising and perhaps alarming before the pandemic, but probably feels more familiar now. Scenario 3 is based on an approach to creative learning that my colleagues at the EdTechTeacher consultancy advocated for when tablet computers first became available. Scenario 4 is inspired by schools that have attempted to develop competency-based or mastery-based approaches to learning, such as Sanborn High School in New Hampshire or the Summit Public Schools in California. None of these approaches is the right answer, but they all have a compelling focus.

As you wrap up thinking about these other possible schools, hopefully they will inspire you and your colleagues to begin to imagine the next level of work for your school or community.

REFINING A VISION: THE SOMEDAY/MONDAY STARTER KIT

PART 1—SOMEDAY: WHAT DOES AWESOME LOOK LIKE?

In the previous chapter, I talked about the Someday/Monday dilemma. Schools need both an ambitious vision to work toward (Someday) and concrete, short-term steps (Monday). The Someday

vision should build on your strengths and areas for growth and imagine ambitious improvements in teaching and learning for your school. The Four Questions for Innovation and the Powerful Learning Environment Activities should help you think about your Someday vision. Over the years, I've discovered that the question "What does awesome look like?" is one creative way to help people start to craft their "Someday" vision of what a classroom, school, or district might look like when they have made substantial progress toward launching innovation.

The "Monday" activities are those steps that can help you take incremental, iterative steps toward that grander vision.

For this activity, stay in a mode of exploration and reflection as you do the following:

1. **Discover and build on previous work.** Have any teachers, students, administrators, community members, or others tried to address your problem of practice (or issues related to it) by experimenting in a school setting? Find out more about these experiments, meaning what happened and how students were impacted. Talk with colleagues, see if you can look at student work, and maybe you can even observe a classroom in action (if relevant). **Engage with a student on their experiences related to your problem of practice.** Students can provide important insights and this kind of interaction could help them feel empowered and connected.

2. Take the time to really **think about "what awesome looks like" for your context and your problem of practice and why it is particularly awesome**. However, this vision should be truly informed by your community, and the school "ecosystem," you inhabit.

   For example, think about equity. Many groups of students are underserved and in need of opportunities that others take for granted. Consider how equity and increasing access to opportunities can be part of your vision of awesome.

3. **Start individually but converge on a shared vision.** As we've seen in this section, refining a vision is not a one-person job. Your vision of change should be informed by the people who will be affected by it. Choose one or two relevant stakeholders to talk to about your vision, especially thinking about student voice. Share what awesome looks like to you and find out what awesome looks like to them. Remember

that learning happens throughout a student's life, not just in a school building. We encourage you to reach out to nontraditional stakeholders within the community to find out what awesome looks like to them. Use these conversations to refine your vision.

PART 2—MONDAY: CONCRETE STEPS

After you have crafted your Someday vision, the next step is to consider concrete steps, complete a step or two, reflect, and plan for future experiments. This is the "Monday" part, meaning actions you can take now(ish) toward realizing your vision. We know there are many questions and details that are still unknown, but every initiative and innovation starts small. The important thing is just to get started.

If you are a teacher, your actions should reflect the inner loop of the Cycle of Experiment and Peer Learning. Think about how you might begin experimenting with instruction, sharing your experiences with your fellow teachers, and talking with administrators about future planning. If you are an administrator, your actions can be inspired by the Cycle of Experiment and Peer Learning. Who do you talk to about increasing support for R&D? How can you formally facilitate teacher sharing?

- Describe one step that you can do by yourself in the next two weeks. Maybe it's as simple as setting up appointments with colleagues you would like to work with.

- Describe one step where input and help from others in your community is likely necessary or desirable. Perhaps you share a memo about your idea with a colleague and ask them about next steps. You can't make change alone; partnerships and collaborations are essential.

- Describe an idea for engaging with students as co-creators. Ideally, students should play a large role in all phases of your initiative.

- Describe an experiment around your problem of practice. This doesn't have to be huge or complex. If you're a teacher, maybe you present content in a different way. If you're an administrator, perhaps you encourage the sharing of student work among teachers in your department. The sooner you can get started trying things, the better.

- Next, consider the impact and result of the steps you wrote about. As you think through each Monday step, take a minute to write down what you think will happen, and how people will respond. You can probably imagine some folks who are ready supporters, and others who will be more skeptical or cautious. When you write down these predictions, it will help you think concretely about what your next steps should entail. But also, some of your predictions will be right and others will be off. People will surprise you, often in positive ways, and it's useful to be able to look back and remember how your predictions compare with your actions. As you take various steps, be sure to record what happened and reflect on it.

As you continue thinking about your Monday steps, all the tools from Design Thinking for Leading and Learning and the Cycle of Experiment and Peer Learning should be helpful here. All those exercises and ideas are about getting to work, trying new things, and sharing what you learned with colleagues, students, and other community members. What the Collaborative Innovation Cycle adds next are strategies for working together through ups and downs, and more tools for measuring progress and adjusting.

ACTIVITIES FOR WORKING TOGETHER THROUGH UPS AND DOWNS

I've facilitated many activities with educators and school leaders, and there is only one where people routinely say during the debrief, "I need to do this with my spouse." This activity, about assumptions and active listening, is a great starting point for teams to work on better communication.

ACTIVITY: LEFT-HAND COLUMN CASE

The Left-Hand Column Case is a tool that allows you to reflect on difficult conversations by charting what was said versus what someone was thinking or feeling. I learned the activity from Peter Senge, and here's how he introduces it:

> *You take a difficult conversation—don't talk about it in the abstract, but a real conversation when you had a certain investment in accomplishing something. You were hopeful that something would occur, and you realized, "This is not working."*
>
> *The Left-Hand Column Case is a reflective tool to dig a little deeper. The basic way it works is that on the right-hand*

side of a piece of paper you write down what was said in a conversation. I said, she said, he said. It could be two people, it could be eight people, doesn't really matter. This is a little bit of what the recording device would record. We would call it the data of the conversation. On the left-hand side of that same piece of paper you write: "What I was thinking or feeling and did not say."

As an example, I walked into the meeting. You know, it's my principal. We had to set aside some time for this issue. I walked in and said, "Gee, I'm really glad you can take the time to do this." She says, "You know, I've only got five minutes." Now, at that point, what do you think is going on in my head? She said, "I've only got five minutes." I immediately go, "Oh, she doesn't care about this thing. We're wasting our time. She never has cared about it. She's always stonewalled." Whatever. I'm off to the races with all kinds of thoughts and feelings. So, when she said that—well, I only have five minutes—I'm over here feeling all this a waste of time. So, I immediately go into hyper mode trying to convince her why this is so important. Rather than having a real genuine conversation, I'm immediately in sales mode. So, you will find that this left-hand column, while it's the invisible part of the conversation, is often the part of the conversation that's driving the conversation.

Instructions:

1 Get into pairs and individually recall a difficult conversation that you have had recently in a professional context, ideally one related to your Someday/Monday vision, or a problem of practice that you and your colleagues hope to work on.

- Give everyone 5–10 minutes to recreate the conversation. Then have everyone take several pieces of paper and draw a line down the center.

2 Right-hand column (what was said).

- In the right-hand column, everyone should write out the dialogue that occurred. The dialogue may go on for several pages. Leave the left-hand column blank until you're finished.

3 Left-hand column (what you were thinking).

- Now in the left-hand column, write out what you were thinking and feeling, but not saying.

4 Paired reflection: Using your left-hand column as a resource:

- Have pairs talk through the scenario. For the person who described the case, take a step back, and look at your left-hand column case as if you were a third-party observer. For the coach, consider some of the following questions:

    - What has really led you to think and feel this way?

    - What was your intention? What were you trying to accomplish?

    - Did you achieve the results you intended?

    - How might your comments have contributed to the difficulties?

    - Why didn't you say what was in your left-hand column?

    - What assumptions are you making about the other person or people?

- What were the costs of operating this way? What were the payoffs?

- What prevented you from acting differently?

- How can you use your left-hand column as a resource to improve your communications?

- Start rewriting the previous conversation as you might have held it. How could your right-hand column (what you said) bring some of your important left-hand column thinking to the surface? How could you have revealed your thoughts in a way that would contribute to the situation turning out the way you wanted? What could you have said that would effectively inquire into the other person's left-hand column?

- Have the coach and discussant switch roles.

5 Share with others.

- Have people in your group pair up and talk about what they've learned together. No one is required to use specifics, name names, or share anything that they feel is too private. Share what you learned by doing this exercise.

Many people find this exercise therapeutic. The debrief often reveal that when conversations go off the rails it might not be because of bad intentions, or irreconcilable differences, or mysterious forces that are causing conflict. Instead, sometimes what causes or drives stressful conversations are unspoken assumptions or thoughts and feelings lurking beneath the surface. Recognizing these underlying emotions feels constructive because seeing and talking about them makes them feel actionable. None of this is magic, of course, and it's very likely that in analyzing these discussions you will find that you still have real differences with the people that you are having hard conversations with. But, as you recognize some of the assumptions or feelings that are driving your parts of the conversation, you may find new handles or pathways toward resolving disagreements in more constructive ways.

ACTIVITIES FOR MEASURING PROGRESS AND ADJUSTING

ASSESSMENT PLANNING SCENARIOS

Over many years of facilitating professional learning with educators, I've found that scenarios, case studies, and even fanciful activities about "other schools" and other places are a good warmup for doing work with your colleagues about your own school. People are keenly aware of the constraints and limitations in their

own contexts, but these limits aren't as salient in new contexts or hypothetical contexts. If you can get educators coming up with new ideas and new approaches in a relatively fast-paced way in a simulation or case study, then that often is a good warmup before working on your own school or context.

When I work with educators on measuring progress and adjusting, I'm typically trying to convince them that with some common sense and disciplined thinking, they can do a better job assessing and monitoring their innovation efforts. In this exercise, I give educators a set of scenarios where they act as consultants, helping an organization figure out how to gather assessment data about a new initiative. After each scenario, I offer a debrief that adds a few power tips assessing new initiatives.

Instructions:

1   Have people in your group pair up. Give each pair an evaluation scenario, making sure that each evaluation scenario is shared by at least two pairs.

2   Have each group read the evaluation scenario and sketch out a plan for assessment according to the prompt on the scenario. Groups should focus not on generating the best idea, but instead on recording what ideas come to mind. Give the groups five to seven minutes.

3   After groups have wrapped up their brainstorming, have them share out and discuss their ideas. Use the following questions to guide your discussion:

   a.   What stakeholders can you include in your assessment plan?

   b.   What are qualitative and quantitative ways of measuring progress?

   c.   How do you measure progress in the short-term or long-term?

   d.   How can you use resources that the school already has to get feedback (e.g., an online parent portal or open house nights)?

   e.   How does assessment look at each stage of the initiative (i.e., before, during, or after)?

f. What is the right scope of assessment (i.e., at the classroom, school, or district level)?

g. What is evidence for change?

SCENARIO 1: SUPPORTING PARENT–TEACHER COMMUNICATION

The lower school at the American School of Brussels is working on increasing connections between home and school and having parents become more aware of, and involved in, their children's classroom experiences. The principal is requiring all elementary teachers to create biweekly classroom newsletters to be emailed to families (beginning in September) to help build these connections. These newsletters will share specifics about lessons and about how the class is doing. **How could you assess, short term and long term (first in October and later in May), whether this initiative is working? Write down at least four ideas.**

Debrief:

So, there are lots of great answers to this exercise. Oftentimes participants will have the idea to look at online log data—are people looking at the newsletters at all? Others will come up with ideas of surveying parents, and I think that's a great idea too. In this first scenario, I usually point out that sometimes people overlook some simple but powerful solutions.

One thing you can do to learn whether an initiative is working is to talk directly to people. Ask your teachers whether they think it's working. Ask parents whether they feel connected to school. Assessment doesn't have to be about quantitative insights; people's subjective experience can be powerful as well. If you are disciplined about taking good notes right after you talk to folks, and thinking carefully about what they are saying, that's also an effective way to start assessing innovation.

SCENARIO 2: CLASSROOM BLOGGING

The Smith School District has launched a districtwide effort to encourage and improve student writing through classroom blogging. They have a districtwide Wordpress installation that makes it easy for teachers and students to start blogging.

Teachers have been encouraged to adopt an approach to student blogging that emphasizes student autonomy, creativity, and attentiveness to a real audience.

The technology director in the school district, Herb Bunt, wants to write his master's thesis about blogging in the district. How should he evaluate whether things are working for students? Write down some ideas.

Debrief:

One of the great things about the Smith School District blogging initiative is that it has clear learning goals for students: to have students exercise autonomy, be creative, and be attentive to a real audience. So that gives us a great sense of what to look for in student work.

As I mentioned previously, Bud Hunt wrote his master's thesis on this very topic in a real school district, so we can look at his action research as a practicing educator. Bud's thesis was a good amount of work, but it's conceptually straightforward. He looked closely at work generated from the blogging initiative. He took a sample of all the posts created in his school blogging system.

Bud noticed that of the 233 blog posts that he sampled, only about 40% were written by students. Students outnumber staff and teachers by something like 10 to 1 in Smith School District, so that suggests that the initiative may not be empowering students as much as one might hope.

Then Bud looked at the kinds of writing that was happening: lots of announcements, lots of assignment responses, lots

(Continued)

of summaries, a little bit of reflection, but not much authentic student writing.

So, by looking closely and systematically at student work, Bud was able to recognize that the goals of the initiative were not well aligned with the work being done by students. Now those are hard findings to have to report out, given all the work that goes into setting something like this up. But it's also how things get better: we try something out, we try to examine in a disciplined way how it's worked, and then we start imagining all the things we might do to make it better. By looking closely at the student work here, Bud gave his district the best possible chance of making good on all their investment and effort. Again, what Bud did was disciplined and systematic, but not impossibly complicated.

If Bud was just starting a pilot blogging exercise with a few classes, it might not be worth doing all this work right away. When things are new and still under development or in pilot, that's a good time to collect people's subjective impressions—which are easy to get and can point you in the right direction. What's great about this example is that Smith School District made a pretty big investment in this effort, so it was worth a very thorough, systematic assessment.

SCENARIO 3: SUPPORTING TEACHER-TO-TEACHER LEARNING

Gail, an assistant principal, heard in a preconference workshop about a practice from another assistant principal: any time one teacher wants to see another teacher's classroom, the interested teacher can just bring a substitute lesson plan, and the principal covers the teacher's class so that observation in another classroom is possible.

This is especially simple when students in the interested teacher's class are taking a test, doing independent project work, and so on.

Gail decides to implement this practice in her school. What should her goals be? How can she know if it's working? Write down some great ideas.

Debrief:

Typically, participants come up with a range of potentially useful goals for this exercise. Some goals might be concrete and near-term, for example, that four teachers would take Gail up on her offer. Others might have a more long-term view of goals—that teachers would conduct more collaborative projects because of their time together in other classrooms. Both might be great goals, and it can be useful to clarify for yourself how you are thinking about the future.

In education, we almost always wrestle with the Someday/Monday dilemma. Often, we have a vision of ambitious changes in teaching and learning that we might be able to achieve someday with a lot of work. But you've got to do something on Monday, and you can't do everything. Separating Someday and Monday can be helpful here. Where do you hope to get one distant day, and what can you get started right now?

One powerful tool in assessment work is prediction. What do you expect to happen? Gail imagines more teacher observation, but what should it lead to? How will it ultimately improve student learning? What's the Someday here? Gail can think about exactly what she's going to do to initiate this new practice. Will she send an email to the faculty? If she does, what does she think will happen? Will people read it? Will they take her seriously? Will they be too busy? Maybe Gail also personally talks to two close teacher colleagues and asks them to take her up on the offer. What will result from that effort?

Predictions and hypotheses can help remind you of your original vision for an initiative. This can be obscured as you get started. So, distinguishing Someday goals from Monday actions, and making predictions as well as planning action steps, can help in this assessment work.

SCENARIO 4: 1-TO-1 PILOT

The Newmarket Elementary School has just purchased 100 tablets to allow them to pilot a 1-to-1 program in the second grade. The director of academic technology is supposed to run the program and then present an evaluation to school leadership at the end of the year. **What questions do you have? Write down at least four ideas.**

Debrief:

There are lots of possible questions, but the best one is: How do you hope student learning will improve because of this investment? How is technology, or any other innovation, in the service of learning?

Especially in education technology, it's common for innovation initiatives to become untethered from their original goals. Innovation in schools is about changing and improving learning experiences for students, but educational technology has so many logistics and details that tech initiatives can often become about power cords, wireless access, single sign-on, and so on, and not about teaching and learning.

When projects head off-track, a great way to try to get them back on track is with assessment. If you ask the question "Is this working?," the next logical question is often "What are we trying to do?" Another way to ask that question is, "What does awesome look like?" If we were successful beyond our wildest dreams, what would we accomplish? How could we measure our progress toward awesome?

It's never too late for assessment. Oftentimes, an effort at assessing innovation can help people refocus on the most important question, which is how our investment in this innovation will make a difference in the learning and in the lives of students.

ASSESSMENT PLAN

If anything is worth doing, it's worth figuring out if you've done it right. For this activity, you'll create an assessment plan that describes how you will measure progress for your initiative. From your Someday/Monday exercise, you've thought about action and impact, so your hypotheses are already on the table. And if your predictions were not correct, that's fine! That's learning. It's reasonable to say, "I've gathered some more data, I've learned a little bit about how this new initiative works, and I'm ready now to try some new things, to predict what will happen, and then to collect some evidence about my results."

For your assessment plan:

- In terms of your initiative, what does positive progress look like? How will you know that you have addressed your problem of practice (at least somewhat), and that you're making progress toward the awesomeness you described earlier in the course? List some indicators, paying special attention to indicators that affect/influence the lives of students. Example: If your problem of practice pertains to a lack of multidisciplinary projects, maybe progress looks like two grade levels attempting at least two projects that involve more than one subject/discipline.

- How will you figure out if these activities are working? What kind of evidence is appropriate? How will you collect it? How will you gather feedback from stakeholders (and which stakeholders are critical)?

- Challenge yourself to go beyond traditional metrics to find other methods/metrics that could help stakeholders understand progress. Take a few minutes to think about whether you could gather data in a way that your school or community hasn't before. Is there a way you could look at two existing data sources together and gain additional insights? Student-centered metrics are especially important. You might include interviews, focus groups, surveys, student work analysis, and so on.

- Change only matters if it affects the day-to-day experience of students and their learning outcomes. How can you include student experiences and student work as you think about what counts as evidence for change? Consider whether students could help collect or interpret data.

FROM LAUNCHING TO SUSTAINING INNOVATION IN SCHOOLS

The magic of our best schools is pretty simple. The places where people are, year after year, making schools better, where they're improving teaching and learning, they're the places where the faculty are having fun, learning, and improving their teaching. When people can find joy in learning with their colleagues, they keep learning. When people find joy in working with their colleagues, they keep collaborating.

Now the beauty of schools that are continuously improving is that they're fabulous learning environments for students. **Students learn more from who we are than from what we tell them.** We know that for students to thrive in a fast-changing and uncertain future, they're going to need to be constantly learning, not just for 12 years, or 16 years, but for their entire lives. And the best way for them to absorb that message is to have them look around at a community of adults who are constantly trying to get better at their jobs, who are constantly trying to make curriculum more powerful and more meaningful, who are constantly finding ways to help students become better versions of themselves.

Hopefully through these chapters, you've launched an innovation. And at some point, by definition, the innovation that you've launched is going to stop being an innovation. After one year, or two years, or four years, or five years, it's not going to be something new anymore. It's just going to be a set of practices. It's going to be the way that you do things. It's going to be a part of the fabric of your teaching and your school life. And it's not going to look exactly like what you imagined when you started. And that's natural. It means that you've been successful in effecting a more permanent change in your school.

When I first started teaching, I'd befriended a colleague named Nick Nickerson. He was the "senior master" at my school, the teacher with the longest tenure, and he was in his thirtieth year teaching math. In the fall of my first year, I asked him, how are your classes going? And he said, "I have three sections that are off and running and doing just great. And there's one that I just haven't figured out yet." I was powerfully struck by that assessment: Nick had 30 years of math teaching experience, and he's still confronted by classes, students, and challenges that he's working on figuring out. For people like Nick, that's the source of ultimate satisfaction in education, the chance to constantly improve craft and improve community.

I hope the tools in this chapter and throughout this book offer new resources and strategies for pursuing that improvement and launching innovation in your schools and environments. And I hope you take as much joy in that work in the years ahead as Nick Nickerson did in his thirtieth year of teaching.

CONCLUSION: CYCLES, ENDINGS, AND BEGINNINGS

BALANCING COHERENCE AND INNOVATION

Good design is about reconciling tensions; here's one last tension. I've argued throughout this book that coherence is one of the signature qualities of our best schools. Coherence means that schools have a shared language for teaching and learning, a common set of right-sized goals that guide their improvement efforts, and processes in place that let different members of the community set the direction for those improvement efforts.

I worked for many years at an extremely coherent summer camp, Camp Chewonki on the coast of Maine. Every few years, we'd make a new marketing video, and it was the easiest communications task in the world. We'd tell the producers to just walk around the camp and interview people, and we'd promise them that they would hear three things repeatedly: that campers and staff felt rich connections to the natural world, that they formed deep communities in their cabins and teams, and that they grew personally as individuals. Of course, people of different ages would express these feelings differently: a young camper might explain that "our counselor helps us fit together like puzzle pieces" and a college-age trip leader might describe the sublime in a morning encounter with a moose, but virtually every unplanned conversation with people in camp would reveal our core values over and over again. Coherence requires a kind of steadiness and stability. It's hard to be coherent when things are constantly changing.

But, as the ancients knew, a rolling stone gathers no moss, and too much coherence for too long leads to stagnation. Ebony Bridwell-Mitchell at the Harvard Graduate School of Education argues that school improvement efforts necessarily follow a cyclical pattern of stability and innovation. To get better, you need periods that are rich with innovation; where a vanguard of teachers launches experiments and then whole teams and faculty participate in intensive periods of iterative refinement and change. These periods that are rich with innovation need to be followed by periods of consolidation, where new innovations become routine practices, and where teaching practices are steady and stable enough to shape institutional culture. "What we do" needs time to become "who we are."[1]

The patterns and timing of these cycles will be very particular to your school. A faculty filled with idealistic young teachers might find that constant innovation is a powerful fuel to their work and mission. As that faculty gets older, has children of their own, and switches from beers after work to aspirin before early bedtimes, the virtues of a more slow and steady approach to longevity may become apparent. As a good guide, iterative innovation needs to feel enriching and adventurous, not an impossible burden atop an already challenging job.

I'm writing this book in 2023, where two years of furious, panicked innovation during the height of the pandemic have been followed by two years of retrenchment, and an understandable desire to get "back to normal," never mind that normal didn't work for too many of our students. I'm hoping that for many educators in many schools, it feels like a fertile time to lean back into innovation. Schools and educators learned many kinds of lessons during the pandemic, but one almost universal lesson was that schools can change much more than we ever thought. So much of what we thought in schools was fixed and permanent turned out to be contingent and flexible.

If we really have to, we can teach without walls, without classrooms, without buses, without blackboards, without schedules, without grades, without curriculum. In 2021, I interviewed a group of educators in Madison, Wisconsin, and one of them told me, "We know how to change. We've changed every three weeks for the past 18 months." The pandemic was brutal, and devastating for many students, but it also helped us discover how much room our schools truly have for change and innovation. I'm hopeful that by the time this book finds its way into your hands, the cycles in your school will align for a period of rich and frequent innovation.

WHEN CYCLES END

A conclusion is the perfect time to talk about endings, so here's one final puzzle of iterative design: When does it end? Throughout this book, I've encouraged you to repeat iterative design cycles and then end those cycles when it feels like the work is ready to transition into a steadier state. But how do you know? How do you know when you have finished a cycle of work, and it's time to move on to new topics and projects? Or when it's time to focus on leading the periods of stability that are important to developing coherence?

I suspect you have discovered by now that the particulars of leading iterative change are ineffable, maybe frustratingly so. In my lab, a huge part of my job is helping new students and new partners judge their cycles of innovation and plan for next steps. It's important for things to fail, and to let ideas that don't prove viable to die on the vine. Failure is freeing; it lets us say goodbye to promising but ineffective approaches and to make room for new ideas. When people learn to trust that failure is part of learning and growing, it's easier to launch experiments, easier to collaborate on someone else's idea, and easier to keep new lines of innovation to a manageable number. Of course, no one who joins my lab feels any of this at the beginning of their time with us: they think that failure feels terrible and *is* terrible. But we make progress with everyone over time.

In my lab, we try to focus on data as our key indicator of the progress of an experiment. What did we say we thought should happen before our playtest? What are the key indicators of success that we defined? Are we seeing progress toward those indicators? How loud was the disconfirming evidence?

But the feelings of the people spearheading an effort are often as important as the evidence. If the lead designer or the design team on a project remains really energized by a new idea, I might let things go longer in the face of mediocre early trials. If the design team seems to be flagging on a new idea, I'm more likely to let a project sunset. Ultimately, our energy and enthusiasm are a vital part of determining how far to push a project when things aren't working.

The broader context matters as well. If there are lots of other good ideas waiting in the wings to try, maybe a new effort gets shelved more quickly in favor of another approach. Sometimes, you will be working on challenges that are vital to a larger problem, something that has to work. I recently heard the new superintendent of Boston Public Schools discuss new ideas for hiring and staffing. In 2022, the labor market was incredibly tight, competition for great educators was fierce, and staff vacancies were at historic highs. The school and district HR teams had to pursue innovations for recruiting and retaining staff because the success of the district depended on it. We might push harder into tough problems in those contexts, as compared with moments where there are multiple viable pathways toward improvement.

As with any part of the design process, conclusions and stopping points are also important times for reflecting and sharing about process. Public sharing opportunities and design critiques are opportunities for your team to reflect on your chosen path, and to imagine the roads not taken—maybe even to saddle up again and return to a road not yet taken.

FINAL THOUGHTS: INCLUSION AND JOY

I have two final reminders for you. One, be bold and persistent in your efforts to be inclusive in your design. When you seek out diverse perspectives, work with diverse teammates, and when you bring folks on the margins into the center of your designs, you will see your work very differently. This is not easy. When you work with your closest colleagues and nearest families, it's quicker to get help, easier to find times to meet, and you avoid the conflict zones that are an inevitable part of working with diverse teams. It will take more time to recruit marginalized folks—make time and space for their genuine contributions and leadership, and work through the ups and downs for collaboration across cultures. And it's all worth it. The purpose of our schools is to create a shared civil society out of our increasingly diverse communities, and the great shame of our schools is the wide gaps in opportunity and achievement that separate our students. The students who are struggling and the families who feel like outsiders have some of the most important answers and ideas to address these challenges. As disability advocates taught us long ago, "Nothing about us without us."

Second, and finally, embrace joyfulness. This work has to be fun. Bring snacks.

The unfortunate reality is that educators are rarely paid extra for improvement work. Determined teachers can close their doors, do their thing, and carry on as they always have. In the schools where continuous improvement is a deep part of the culture, teachers describe collaboration as one of the most enjoyable parts of the job. The deep care for children that defines most teachers is made manifest in efforts to make learning better. Our scholarly love of the disciplines and of learning finds expression in systemic, empirical efforts to creatively improve our teaching. If you don't know what to do next in your improvement work, a powerful question to return to is simply: "What would be fun?"

I get a jolt of energy every time I visit a school where exciting things are happening. A major part of what I teach my undergraduates at MIT is that teaching and learning are infinitely fascinating. In the marvelous workings of our classrooms, we witness the impossibly complex interactions of design, tradition, culture, innovation, biology, psychology, technology, and sociology in 42-minute periods. In an educator's life, you will never run out of things to learn, of lessons to improve, of relationships to deepen, of minds to watch blossom. I hope the ideas in this book give you new ways to explore those mysteries, and new joys to find in making your schools and classrooms flourish.

ABOUT THE AUTHOR

Justin is an associate professor of digital media in the Comparative Media Studies/Writing department at MIT and the director of the Teaching Systems Lab. He is the author of *Failure to Disrupt: Why Technology Alone Can't Transform Education*, and the host of the TeachLab podcast. He earned his doctorate from the Harvard Graduate School of Education. He is a past Fellow at the Berkman-Klein Center for Internet and Society. His writings have been published in *Science*, *Proceedings of the National Academy of Sciences*, *Washington Post*, *The Atlantic*, and other scholarly journals and public venues. He started his career as a high school history teacher and coach of wrestling and outdoor adventure activities.

NOTES

INTRODUCTION: THE SECRET TO SCHOOL IMPROVEMENT

1. Benjamin Erwin, *Creative Projects with Lego Mindstorms* (Addison-Wesley Professional, 2001).

CHAPTER 1: WHAT IS THE CYCLE OF EXPERIMENT AND PEER LEARNING?

1. Justin Reich, *Failure to Disrupt: Why Technology Alone Can't Transform Education* (Harvard University Press, 2020).
2. When I visit schools as part of a formal research study, I typically agree to keep the school anonymous or pseudonymous in subsequent writing. The schools that I name specifically either came to my attention through consulting work or informal connections.
3. John B. Diamond, "Where the Rubber Meets the Road: Rethinking the Connection between High-Stakes Testing Policy and Classroom Instruction," *Sociology of Education* 80, no. 4 (2007): 285–313.
4. Ebony N. Bridwell-Mitchell, "Theorizing Teacher Agency and Reform: How Institutionalized Instructional Practices Change and Persist," *Sociology of Education* 88, no. 2 (2015): 140–159.

5. OECD, "Indicator D4: How much time do teachers spend teaching?," in *Education at a Glance 2014: OECD Indicators* (OECD Publishing, 2014), http://dx.doi.org/10.1787/888933120005.

6. The best summary of Professor Senge's work in schools is Peter M. Senge, Nelda Cambron-McCabe, Timothy Lucas, Bryan Smith, and Janis Dutton, *Schools That Learn (Updated and Revised): A Fifth Discipline Fieldbook for Educators, Parents, and Everyone Who Cares About Education* (Currency, 2012).

7. Ilana Horn and Brette Garner, *Teacher Learning of Ambitious and Equitable Mathematics Instruction: A Sociocultural Approach* (Routledge, 2022).

8. One of the best meditations on loss and change in school is Robert Evans, *The Human Side of School Change: Reform, Resistance, and the Real-Life Problems of Innovation* (San Francisco, CA: Jossey-Bass, 1996).

9. Justin Reich, "Conflict and Identity: Using Contemporary Questions to Inspire the Study of the Past," *World History Connected*, February 2007, https://worldhistoryconnected.press.uillinois.edu/4.2/reich.html.

10. Jeannie Oakes, *Keeping Track: How Schools Structure Inequality* (Yale University Press, 2005).

11. One of the best starting points on digital divides with education technology is Paul Attewell, "Comment: The First and Second Digital Divides," *Sociology of Education* 74, no. 3 (2001): 252–259.

12. Karl E. Weick, "Educational Organizations as Loosely Coupled Systems," *Administrative Science Quarterly* (1976): 1–19.

CHAPTER 2: SPINNING THE CYCLE OF EXPERIMENT AND PEER LEARNING

1. Martha Stone Wiske, "A Cultural Perspective on School–University Collaboration," in David Perkins and Judah Schwartz, eds., *Software Goes to School: Teaching for Understanding with New Technologies* (Oxford University Press, 1995), 187–212.

2. Louise Bay Waters, superintendent of the Leadership Public Schools, described this work at a Hewlett Foundation meeting in 2011, and her remarks were archived at https://blog.ck12info.org/oer-presentation-dr-louise-waters-leadership-public-schools/.

3. The US Department of Education's Office of Educational Technology has an overview of Burlington's efforts at https://tech.ed.gov/stories/students-as-tech-support/.

4. Katie Salen Tekinbas, Robert Torres, Loretta Wolozin, Rebecca Rufo-Tepper, and Arana Shapiro, *Quest to Learn: Developing the School for Digital Kids* (MIT Press, 2010).

5. Tom Daccord and Justin Reich, *iPads in the Classroom: From Consumption to Curation and Creation* (Learning Sciences International, 2015).

6. Eric Buchovechy, *ATLAS: Learning From Student Work,* National School Reform Faculty, https://www.nsrfharmony.org/wp-content/uploads/2017/10/atlas_lfsw_0.pdf.

7. Elizabeth A. City, Richard F. Elmore, Sarah E. Fiarman, and Lee Teitel, *Instructional Rounds in Education*, vol. 30 (Cambridge, MA: Harvard Education Press, 2009).

8. Andy Jacob and Kate McGovern, "The Mirage: Confronting the Hard Truth about Our Quest for Teacher Development," *TNTP* (2015).

9.   Justin Reich and Dan Callahan, "Tired of PD? Try an Edcamp," *Harvard Education Letter* 28, no. 5 (September/October 2012), http://www.hepg.org/hel/article/549.

10.   Daccord and Reich, *iPads in the Classroom.*

11.   For more on the importance of teacher autonomy and agency in professional learning, see James Noonan, "An Affinity for Learning: Teacher Identity and Powerful Professional Development," *Journal of Teacher Education* 70, no. 5 (2019): 526–537.

12.   Grant Wiggins and Jay McTighe, *Understanding by Design* (ASCD, 2005); Martha Stone Wiske, *Teaching for Understanding: Linking Research with Practice* (San Francisco: Jossey-Bass, 1998); Tracey E. Hall, Anne Meyer, and David H. Rose, eds., *Universal Design for Learning in the Classroom: Practical Applications* (Guilford Press, 2012); Doug Lemov, *Teach Like a Champion: 49 Techniques That Put Students on the Path to College* (John Wiley & Sons, 2010).

13.   Jal Mehta and Sarah Fine, *In Search of Deeper Learning: The Quest to Remake the American High School* (Harvard University Press, 2019).

CHAPTER 3: WHAT IS DESIGN THINKING?

1.   Jessica Lahey, "How Design Thinking Became a Buzzword at School," *The Atlantic*, January 4, 2017.

2.   One of the classic early texts in software engineering that presaged the transition from Waterfall to Agile approaches is Frederick P. Brooks, *The Mythical Man-Month: Essays on Software Engineering* (Addison-Wesley Longman, 1992).

3. As of this writing, this terrific piece of web history is still live at https://www.kickstarter.com/projects/darkpony/drawing-for-dollars.

4. Richard Buchanan, "Wicked Problems in Design Thinking," *Design Issues* 8, no. 2 (1992): 5–21.

5. John Dewey, "My Pedagogic Creed," *School Journal* 54, no. 3 (1897): 77–80.

6. Chris Lehmann and Zac Chase, *Building School 2.0: How to Create the Schools We Need* (San Francisco, CA: John Wiley & Sons, 2015).

7. Sasha Costanza-Chock, *Design Justice: Community-Led Practices to Build the Worlds We Need* (Cambridge, MA: MIT Press, 2020).

8. James I. Charlton, *Nothing About Us Without Us* (Oakland, CA: University of California Press, 1998).

9. Herbert A. Simon, *The Sciences of the Artificial* (Cambridge, MA: MIT Press, 2019).

10. Dan Silver, Anna Saavedra, and Morgan Polikoff, "Low Parent Interest in COVID-Recovery Interventions Should Worry Educators and Policymakers Alike," *Brookings Brown Center Chalkboard*, Brookings, August 16, 2022, https://www.brookings.edu/blog/brown-center-chalkboard/2022/08/16/low-parent-interest-in-covid-recovery-interventions-should-worry-educators-and-policymakers-alike/.

11. Justin Reich and Jal Mehta, "Imagining September: Principles and Design Elements for Ambitious Schools During COVID-19" (2020), https://edarxiv.org/gqa2w.

12. Jos Boys, *Doing Disability Differently: An Alternative Handbook on Architecture, Dis/ability and Designing for Everyday Life* (Routledge, 2014). Another good resource on designing for variation is Todd Rose, *The End of Average: How to Succeed in a World That Values Sameness* (Penguin UK, 2016).

13. Judy Halbert and Linda Kaser, *Leading Through Spirals of Inquiry: For Equity and Quality* (Portage & Main Press, 2022).

CHAPTER 4: GETTING STARTED WITH DESIGN

1. Richard Milner, *Start Where You Are, But Don't Stay There* (Cambridge, MA: Harvard Education Press, 2021).
2. A readable summary of key ideas is John R. Rossiter and Gary L. Lilien, "New 'Brainstorming' Principles," *Australian Journal of Management* 19, no. 1 (1994): 61–72.
3. If you are interested, you can print and play the materials for Baldermath at https://tsl.mit.edu/practice_space/baldermath/.

CHAPTER 5: WHAT IS THE COLLABORATIVE INNOVATION CYCLE?

1. The inveterate Quote Investigator traces the history of the saying here: https://quoteinvestigator.com/2012/01/24/future-has-arrived/.
2. Peter Senge, *The Fifth Discipline: The Art and Practice of the Learning Organization* (Random House Business Books, 1992).
3. See for instance, Barbara Mellers, Ralph Hertwig, and Daniel Kahneman, "Do Frequency Representations Eliminate Conjunction Effects? An Exercise in Adversarial Collaboration," *Psychological Science* 12, no. 4 (2001): 269–275.

CONCLUSION: CYCLES, ENDINGS, AND BEGINNINGS

1. Ebony N. Bridwell-Mitchell, "Theorizing Teacher Agency and Reform: How Institutionalized Instructional Practices Change and Persist," *Sociology of Education* 88, no. 2 (2015): 140–159.

INDEX